# MathFlare

**Name:** _______________________

**Class:** ___________

**Teacher:** _______________________

# Introduction

As parents and educators, we recognize the pivotal role mathematics plays in shaping a child's academic journey and future success. Yet, the path to mathematical proficiency can often seem daunting, fraught with challenges and complexities. That's where the transformative power of MathFlare Workbooks shine through, illuminating the way forward with clarity, precision, and purpose.

Introducing MathFlare Workbooks – a beacon of guidance, a testament to excellence, and a catalyst for achievement. Crafted with meticulous care and expertise, MathFlare Workbooks stand as paragons of educational excellence, designed to nurture young minds, ignite a passion for learning, and develop a deep-rooted understanding of mathematical concepts.

Picture this: your child eagerly delves into the pages of Mathflare Workbook, greeted by a step-by-step guide illuminated with vivid examples that demystify complex mathematical concepts. With each turn of the page, they embark on a journey of discovery, encountering thoughtfully curated practice questions that reinforce learning and hone problem-solving skills. And when they unveil the answers to those very questions, a sense of accomplishment blossoms within them – a tangible reward for their hard work and dedication.

But MathFlare Workbooks are more than just tools for learning; they are pathways to comprehension, fostering a deep-seated understanding of mathematical concepts through a sequential, logical flow. From fundamental principles to advanced problem-solving strategies, every chapter builds upon the last, ensuring a robust foundation upon which future knowledge can be constructed.

As parents, we yearn for nothing more than to see our children thrive, to witness the spark of inspiration ignited within them as they conquer academic challenges with confidence and poise. MathFlare Workbooks serve as partners in this noble endeavor, offering not just practice questions, but the keys to unlocking a world of opportunity.

And for teachers, MathFlare Workbooks stand as invaluable allies in the quest to cultivate mathematical proficiency in the classroom. With answers readily available, instructors can focus on guiding and nurturing their students, confident in the knowledge that MathFlare Workbooks provide a solid framework upon which to build.

In the pages of MathFlare Workbooks, we find not just the promise of academic excellence, but the seeds of a brighter tomorrow. So let us embrace the power of mathematics, let us champion the journey of learning, and let us pave the way for a generation of young minds poised to shape the world. With MathFlare Workbooks as our guide, the possibilities are infinite, and the future, bright.

# Table of Contents

MathFlare
Grade 2
MATH WORKBOOK
Step by Step Guide and Essential Practice with Answers
Addition Subtraction
Multiplication
Place Value and Expanded Notations
Geometry
MathFlare Publishing

MathFlare
Grade 2-3
MATH WORKBOOK
Step by Step Guide and Essential Practice with Answers
Addition Subtraction
Multiplication and Division
Place Value and Expanded Notations
Geometry
MathFlare Publishing

MathFlare
Grade 3
MATH WORKBOOK
Step by Step Guide and Essential Practice with Answers
Multiplication and Division
Decimals
Place Value and Expanded Notations
Fractions and Geometry
MathFlare Publishing

MathFlare
Grade 1
MATH WORKBOOK
Step by Step Guide and Essential Practice with Answers
Counting and Numbers
Addition and Subtraction
Place Value and Expanded Notations
Understanding Time
MathFlare Publishing

MathFlare
Grade 1-2
MATH WORKBOOK
Step by Step Guide and Essential Practice with Answers
Counting and Numbers
Addition and Subtraction
Place Value and Expanded Notations
Understanding Time
MathFlare Publishing

MathFlare
Grade 3-4
MATH WORKBOOK
Step by Step Guide and Essential Practice with Answers
Addition Subtraction
Multiplication Division
Place Value and Expanded Notations
Fractions and Geometry
MathFlare Publishing

MathFlare
Grade 4
MATH WORKBOOK
Step by Step Guide and Essential Practice with Answers
Addition Subtraction
Multiplication Division
Place Value and Expanded Notations
Fractions and Geometry
MathFlare Publishing

MathFlare
Grade 4-5
MATH WORKBOOK
Step by Step Guide and Essential Practice with Answers
Multiplication Division
Place Value and Expanded Notations
Fractions and Geometry
Unit Conversion
MathFlare Publishing

MathFlare
MATH
WORKBOOK
Grade 5
Step by Step Guide
and Essential Practice
with Answers
Multiplication
Division
Place Value and
Expanded
Notations
Fractions
and Geometry
Unit
Conversion
MathFlare Publishing

MathFlare
MATH
WORKBOOK
Grade 5-6
Step by Step Guide
and Essential Practice
with Answers
Multiplication
Division
Place Value and
Expanded
Notations
Fractions
and Geometry
Units and
Statistics
MathFlare Publishing

MathFlare
MATH
WORKBOOK
Grade 6
Step by Step Guide
and Essential Practice
with Answers
Integers and
Statistics
Arithmetic and
Pre-Algebra
Fractions
and Geometry
Ratio and
Percentage
MathFlare Publishing

MathFlare
MATH
WORKBOOK
Grade 6-7
Step by Step Guide
and Essential Practice
with Answers
Arithmetic and
Pre-Algebra
Ratio, Percent
Proportion
Geometry
Statistics
MathFlare Publishing

MathFlare
MATH
WORKBOOK
Grade 7
Step by Step Guide
and Essential Practice
with Answers
Pre-Algebra
Ratio, Percent
Proportion
Geometry
Statistics
MathFlare Publishing

MathFlare
MATH
WORKBOOK
Grade 7-8
Step by Step Guide
and Essential Practice
with Answers
Pre-Algebra
Ratio, Percent
Proportion
Geometry and
Cartesian
Plane
Statistics
MathFlare Publishing

MathFlare
MATH
WORKBOOK
Grade 8-9
Step by Step Guide
and Essential Practice
with Answers
Pre-Algebra
Ratio, Proportion
and Percentage
Linear
Equations
Geometry and
Cartesian Plane
MathFlare Publishing

MathFlare
MATH
WORKBOOK
Grade 8
Step by Step Guide
and Essential Practice
with Answers
Pre-Algebra
Percentage
Linear
Equations
Geometry
MathFlare Publishing

# Addition and Subtraction

## Addition with Regrouping

When we do addition, we combine numbers. But sometimes, when we're adding numbers, we might need to regroup. Regrouping means we have to move a number from one place to another, usually to the next column, to get the right answer.

For Example: Let's take an example of adding 6533 and 7579 together:

$$6\ 5\ 3\ 3$$
$$+7\ 5\ 7\ 9$$

First, we start by adding the digits in the ones place: 3 + 9 = 12. We write down the 2 in the ones place and carry over the 1 to the tens place.

$$1$$
$$6\ 5\ 3\ 3$$
$$+7\ 5\ 7\ 9$$
$$2$$

Now, we add the digits in the tens place, along with the carry-over: 3 + 7 + 1 = 11. We write down the 1 in the tens place and carry over the 1 to the hundreds place.

$$1\ 1$$
$$6\ 5\ 3\ 3$$
$$+7\ 5\ 7\ 9$$
$$1\ 2$$

Now, we add the digits in the hundreds place, along with the carry-over: 5 + 5 + 1 = 11. We write down the 1 in the tens place and carry over the 1 to the hundreds place.

$$
\begin{array}{r}
1\ 1\ 1\phantom{0} \\
6\ 5\ 3\ 3 \\
+7\ 5\ 7\ 9 \\
\hline
1\ 1\ \ 2
\end{array}
$$

Now, we add the digits in the thousandth place, along with the carry-over: 6 + 7 + 1 = 14.

$$
\begin{array}{r}
1\ 1\ 1\phantom{0} \\
6\ 5\ 3\ 3 \\
+7\ 5\ 7\ 9 \\
\hline
1\ 4\ 1\ 1\ 2
\end{array}
$$

This process of carrying over helps us accurately add numbers, especially when they're larger.

## Subtraction with Regrouping

Subtraction is a key math operation where we find the difference between two numbers. Sometimes, when we subtract, we might need to regroup, which means borrowing from the next column.

Let's take an example of subtracting 8436 from 6563:

First, we start by subtracting the digits in the ones place: 3 - 6.

Since 3 is less than 6, we need to regroup. We borrow 1 from the tens place, making it 5 tens instead of 6, and add it to the ones place.

So, 3 becomes 13, and then we subtract 6.

$$\begin{array}{r} 8\ 5\ 6\ ^{1}3 \\ -6\ 4\ 3\ 6 \\ \hline 7 \end{array}$$

Now, we subtract the tens place digits: 5 - 3 = 2

$$\begin{array}{r} 5 \\ 8\ 5\ \cancel{6}\ ^{1}3 \\ -6\ 4\ 3\ 6 \\ \hline 2\ 7 \end{array}$$

Now, we subtract the hundreds place digits: 5 - 4 = 1

$$\begin{array}{r} 5 \\ 8\ 5\ \cancel{6}\ ^{1}3 \\ -6\ 4\ 3\ 6 \\ \hline 1\ 2\ 7 \end{array}$$

Now, we subtract the hundreds place digits: 8 - 6 = 2

$$\begin{array}{r} 5 \\ 8\ 5\ \cancel{6}\ ^{1}3 \\ -6\ 4\ 3\ 6 \\ \hline 2\ 1\ 2\ 7 \end{array}$$

This process of regrouping or borrowing helps us accurately subtract numbers, especially when the top digit is smaller than the bottom one.

Let's solve problems from exercises:

$$\begin{array}{r} 6{,}133 \\ +\ 9{,}978 \\ \hline 16{,}111 \end{array} \qquad \begin{array}{r} 6{,}650 \\ -\ 5{,}798 \\ \hline 852 \end{array}$$

# Word Problems

Word problems are like little puzzles that help us use addition in real-life situations.

For instance:

1. Jake has 6 carrots. He gets 2 more carrots. How many carrots does he have now?

To find out how many carrots he has now, we add the number of carrots he started with (6) to the number of carrots he got (2).

So, we add 6 + 2, which equals 8. Jake now has 8 carrots in total!

2. Jake saved up 4 dollars to buy pencils. He spent 2 dollars on it. How much money does he have left?

To solve this problem, we need to start with the number of dollars Jake started with and subtract the number of dollars he spent on the pencils.

So, we subtract 2 from 4, which equals 2: Jake has 2 dollars left after buying the pencils.

We need to understand what the problem is asking and what information it provides. Then, we can use addition or subtraction, depending on whether we're combining or taking away objects, to find the answer.

Let's solve problems from exercises:

Ayden bought a pair of shoes for 32 dollars. Later, Ayden bought another pair of shoes for 60 dollars. How much money did Ayden spend in total??

$$\begin{array}{rl} \$32 & \text{spent on 1st pair of shoes} \\ +\ \$60 & \text{spent on another pair of shoes} \\ \hline \$92 & \text{Ayden spent in total} \end{array}$$

Sandra has 38 bananas. She ate 29 of them. How many bananas does Sandra have left?

$$\begin{array}{r} 38 \\ -\ 29 \\ \hline 9 \end{array}$$

Sandra had 38 bananas

She ate 29 of them

she has 9 bananas left

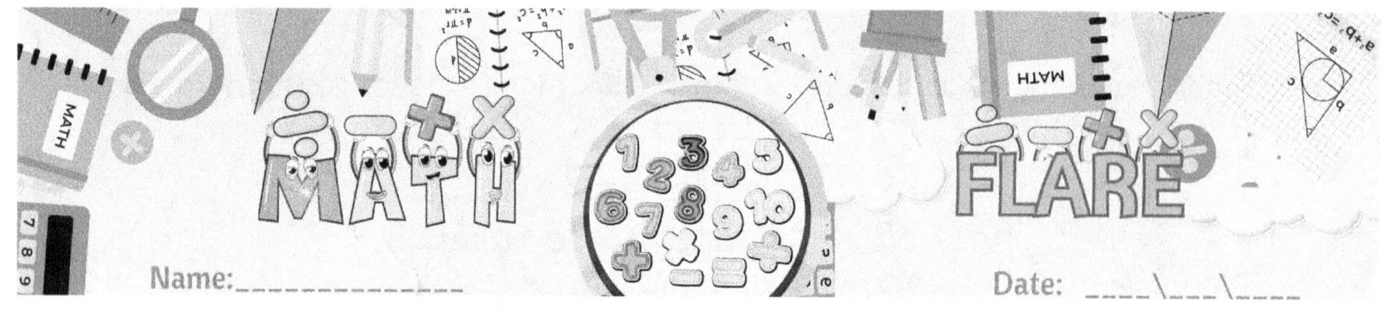

# Addition with Regrouping

Find the sum.

| | | | |
|---|---|---|---|
| 1.    9,422<br>+ 7,898 | 2.    3,451<br>+ 8,669 | 3.    3,849<br>+ 8,588 | 4.    6,791<br>+ 8,559 |
| 5.    3,863<br>+ 8,798 | 6.    4,612<br>+ 7,598 | 7.    1,316<br>+ 9,799 | 8.    3,174<br>+ 8,997 |
| 9.    6,156<br>+ 5,995 | 10.    4,434<br>+ 9,796 | 11.    1,118<br>+ 9,993 | 12.    2,862<br>+ 9,299 |
| 13.    9,981<br>+ 7,779 | 14.    5,375<br>+ 8,956 | 15.    6,316<br>+ 8,895 | 16.    9,421<br>+ 9,999 |
| 17.    2,285<br>+ 8,897 | 18.    9,134<br>+ 1,977 | 19.    4,968<br>+ 8,948 | 20.    7,593<br>+ 4,867 |

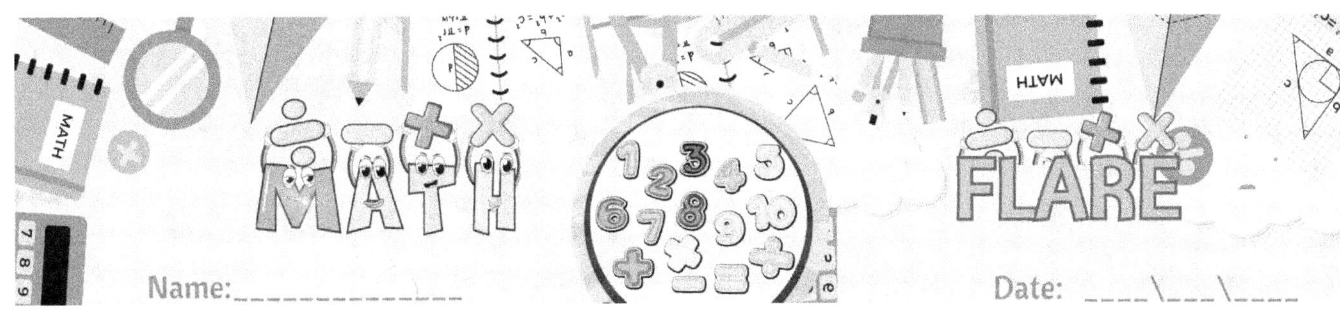



Name:_________________          Date: ___________

| | | | |
|---|---|---|---|
| 21.  5,161<br>+ 8,969 | 22.  1,264<br>+ 9,999 | 23.  5,412<br>+ 7,699 | 24.  2,417<br>+ 8,696 |
| 25.  5,662<br>+ 7,479 | 26.  1,786<br>+ 9,695 | 27.  3,235<br>+ 8,987 | 28.  2,967<br>+ 9,779 |
| 29.  5,231<br>+ 7,979 | 30.  1,486<br>+ 9,776 | 31.  1,213<br>+ 9,997 | 32.  3,252<br>+ 8,989 |
| 33.  4,373<br>+ 8,999 | 34.  3,943<br>+ 7,768 | 35.  6,467<br>+ 8,777 | 36.  8,621<br>+ 4,899 |
| 37.  7,551<br>+ 9,579 | 38.  5,481<br>+ 7,989 | 39.  3,439<br>+ 7,971 | 40.  1,791<br>+ 9,849 |

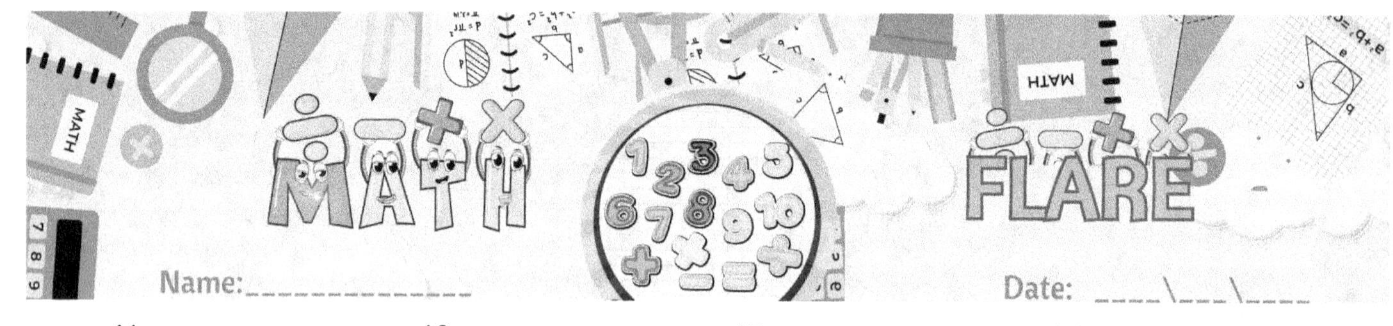



| | | | |
|---|---|---|---|
| 41.   6,371<br>+ 6,839 | 42.   3,591<br>+ 9,839 | 43.   8,169<br>+ 8,968 | 44.   7,173<br>+ 7,949 |
| 45.   6,629<br>+ 6,496 | 46.   6,216<br>+ 7,999 | 47.   2,432<br>+ 8,888 | 48.   4,647<br>+ 6,585 |
| 49.   5,851<br>+ 6,259 | 50.   7,117<br>+ 3,999 | 51.   1,195<br>+ 9,998 | 52.   8,588<br>+ 3,925 |
| 53.   8,553<br>+ 7,667 | 54.   4,739<br>+ 8,671 | 55.   9,699<br>+ 1,962 | 56.   4,281<br>+ 7,869 |
| 57.   6,458<br>+ 4,663 | 58.   9,711<br>+ 9,899 | 59.   5,946<br>+ 5,177 | 60.   6,936<br>+ 6,275 |

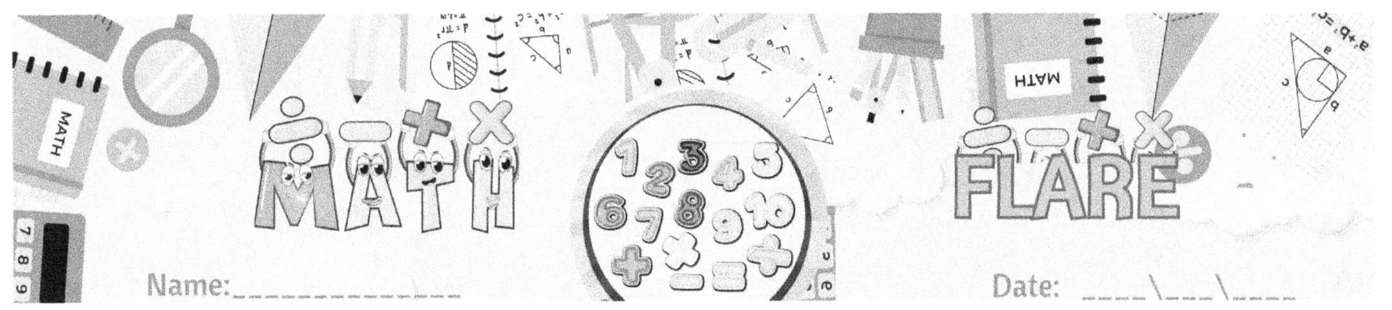



Name: _______________     Date: ___/___/___

| | | | |
|---|---|---|---|
| 61.   8,219<br>+ 6,899 | 62.   6,178<br>+ 4,952 | 63.   6,531<br>+ 7,999 | 64.   2,716<br>+ 8,599 |
| 65.   5,926<br>+ 8,987 | 66.   7,153<br>+ 7,988 | 67.   5,253<br>+ 9,977 | 68.   6,646<br>+ 6,676 |
| 69.   2,731<br>+ 9,699 | 70.   1,578<br>+ 9,772 | 71.   4,391<br>+ 8,719 | 72.   7,414<br>+ 6,697 |
| 73.   9,135<br>+ 3,986 | 74.   2,262<br>+ 9,988 | 75.   2,819<br>+ 8,793 | 76.   1,576<br>+ 9,735 |
| 77.   9,319<br>+ 1,895 | 78.   2,899<br>+ 9,355 | 79.   4,621<br>+ 6,589 | 80.   7,393<br>+ 7,759 |

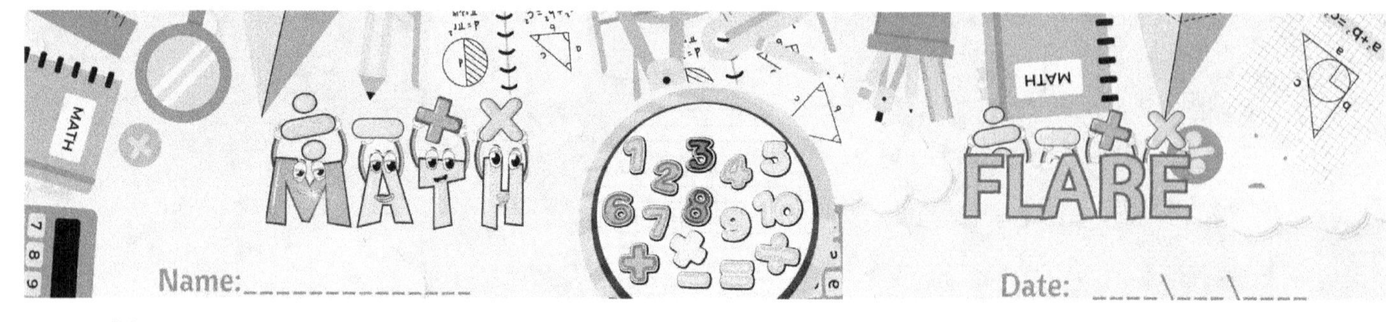


| | | | |
|---|---|---|---|
| 81.  5,942<br>+ 8,768 | 82.  7,735<br>+ 3,795 | 83.  4,118<br>+ 7,997 | 84.  8,616<br>+ 5,796 |
| 85.  7,996<br>+ 4,438 | 86.  8,163<br>+ 6,987 | 87.  3,542<br>+ 8,579 | 88.  2,851<br>+ 8,869 |
| 89.  9,434<br>+ 9,989 | 90.  4,916<br>+ 7,195 | 91.  9,638<br>+ 4,987 | 92.  4,211<br>+ 6,999 |
| 93.  8,381<br>+ 5,829 | 94.  7,861<br>+ 4,379 | 95.  8,771<br>+ 3,899 | 96.  3,151<br>+ 7,999 |
| 97.  3,272<br>+ 7,969 | 98.  5,479<br>+ 5,682 | 99.  6,676<br>+ 6,667 | 100.  3,559<br>+ 7,768 |

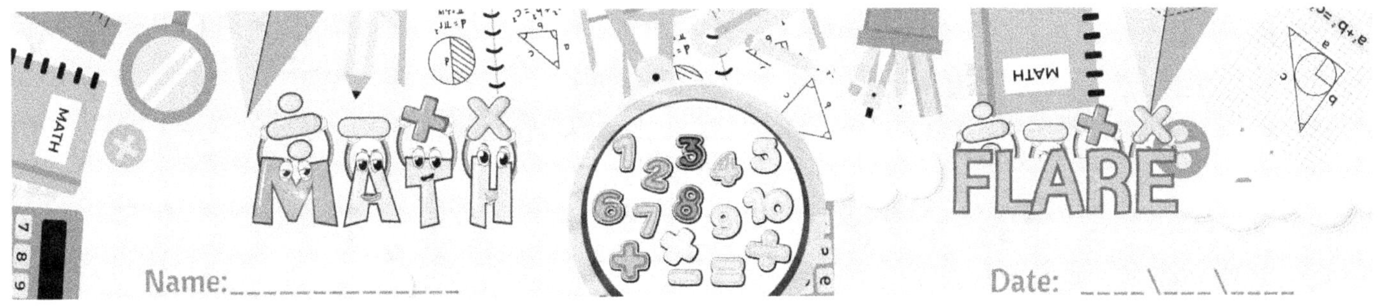

# Subtraction with Regrouping

Find the difference.

| | | | |
|---|---|---|---|
| 101.    4,738<br>− 3,979 | 102.    9,781<br>− 8,998 | 103.    6,588<br>− 3,699 | 104.    9,188<br>− 3,599 |
| 105.    9,023<br>− 7,358 | 106.    4,821<br>− 2,995 | 107.    2,621<br>− 1,882 | 108.    8,012<br>− 1,799 |
| 109.    5,488<br>− 3,799 | 110.    4,361<br>− 3,496 | 111.    9,235<br>− 4,879 | 112.    7,014<br>− 4,149 |
| 113.    2,878<br>− 1,999 | 114.    4,008<br>− 3,889 | 115.    2,035<br>− 1,769 | 116.    8,131<br>− 3,997 |

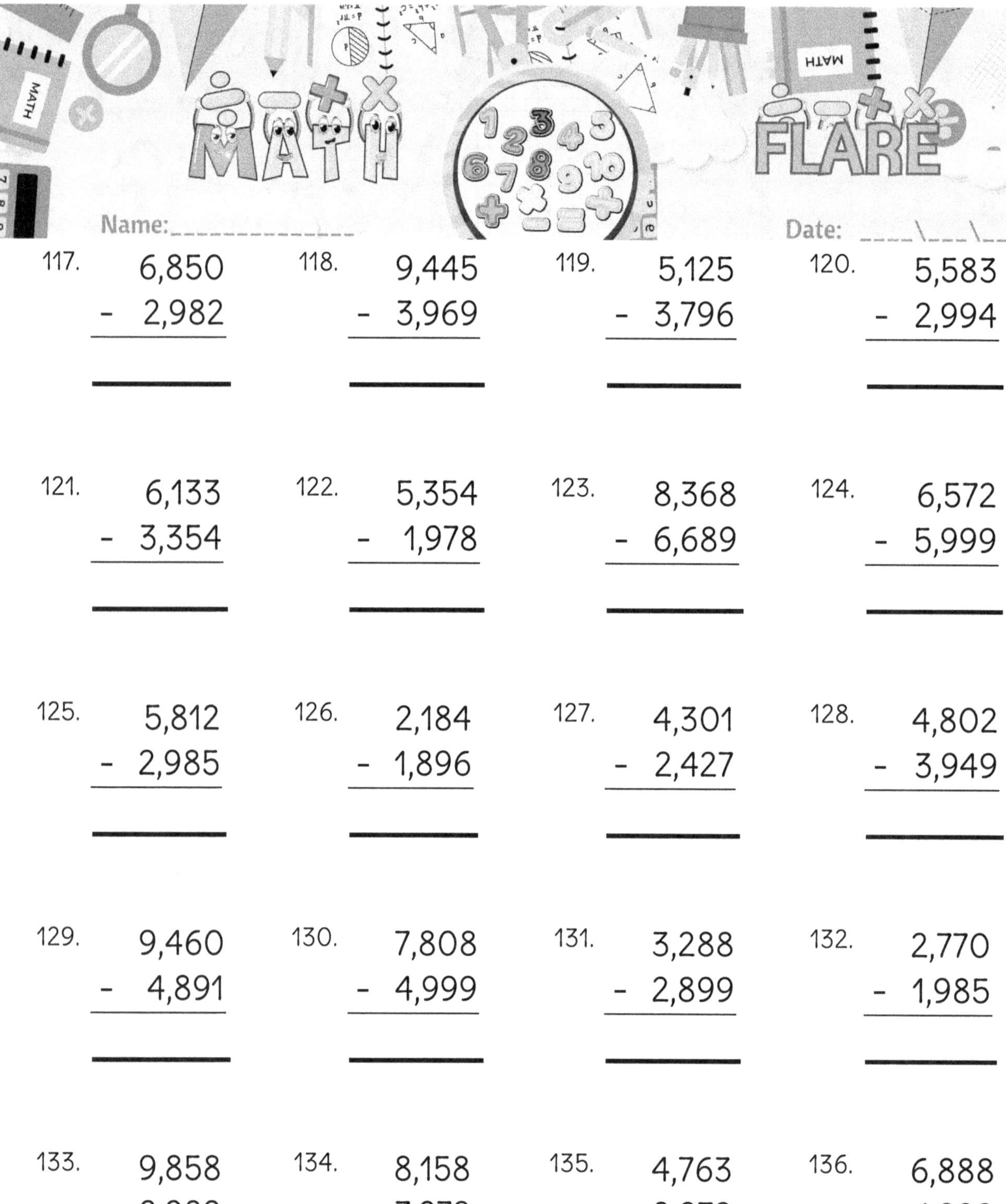

Name:______________________    Date: _______________

| | | | |
|---|---|---|---|
| 117.   6,850 <br> − 2,982 | 118.   9,445 <br> − 3,969 | 119.   5,125 <br> − 3,796 | 120.   5,583 <br> − 2,994 |
| 121.   6,133 <br> − 3,354 | 122.   5,354 <br> − 1,978 | 123.   8,368 <br> − 6,689 | 124.   6,572 <br> − 5,999 |
| 125.   5,812 <br> − 2,985 | 126.   2,184 <br> − 1,896 | 127.   4,301 <br> − 2,427 | 128.   4,802 <br> − 3,949 |
| 129.   9,460 <br> − 4,891 | 130.   7,808 <br> − 4,999 | 131.   3,288 <br> − 2,899 | 132.   2,770 <br> − 1,985 |
| 133.   9,858 <br> − 2,989 | 134.   8,158 <br> − 7,279 | 135.   4,763 <br> − 2,879 | 136.   6,888 <br> − 1,999 |

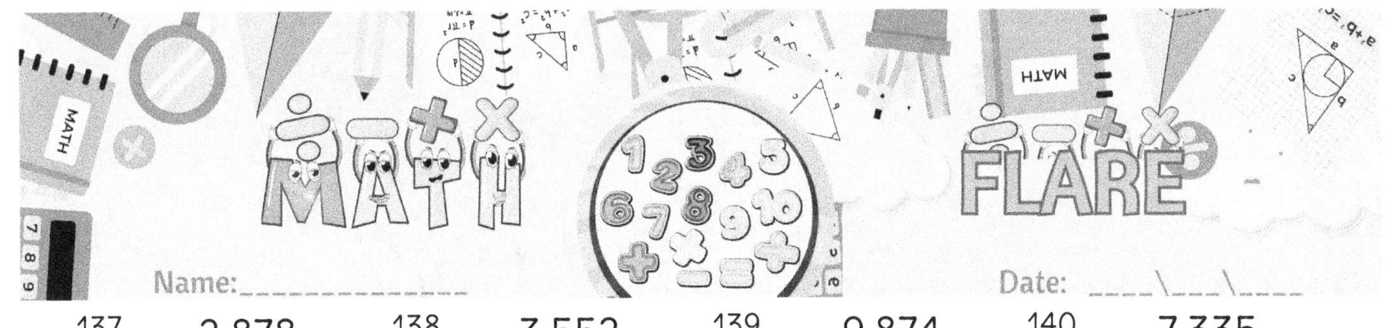


| | | | |
|---|---|---|---|
| 137.  2,878<br>−  1,989 | 138.  3,552<br>−  2,685 | 139.  9,874<br>−  6,988 | 140.  7,335<br>−  3,858 |
| 141.  5,388<br>−  2,999 | 142.  4,703<br>−  3,868 | 143.  6,885<br>−  5,997 | 144.  9,470<br>−  2,995 |
| 145.  9,075<br>−  8,598 | 146.  4,702<br>−  1,816 | 147.  8,611<br>−  7,785 | 148.  3,786<br>−  2,998 |
| 149.  3,287<br>−  1,699 | 150.  2,723<br>−  1,867 | 151.  9,781<br>−  7,894 | 152.  5,288<br>−  1,599 |
| 153.  7,554<br>−  1,677 | 154.  9,134<br>−  4,698 | 155.  3,321<br>−  2,539 | 156.  9,634<br>−  4,966 |

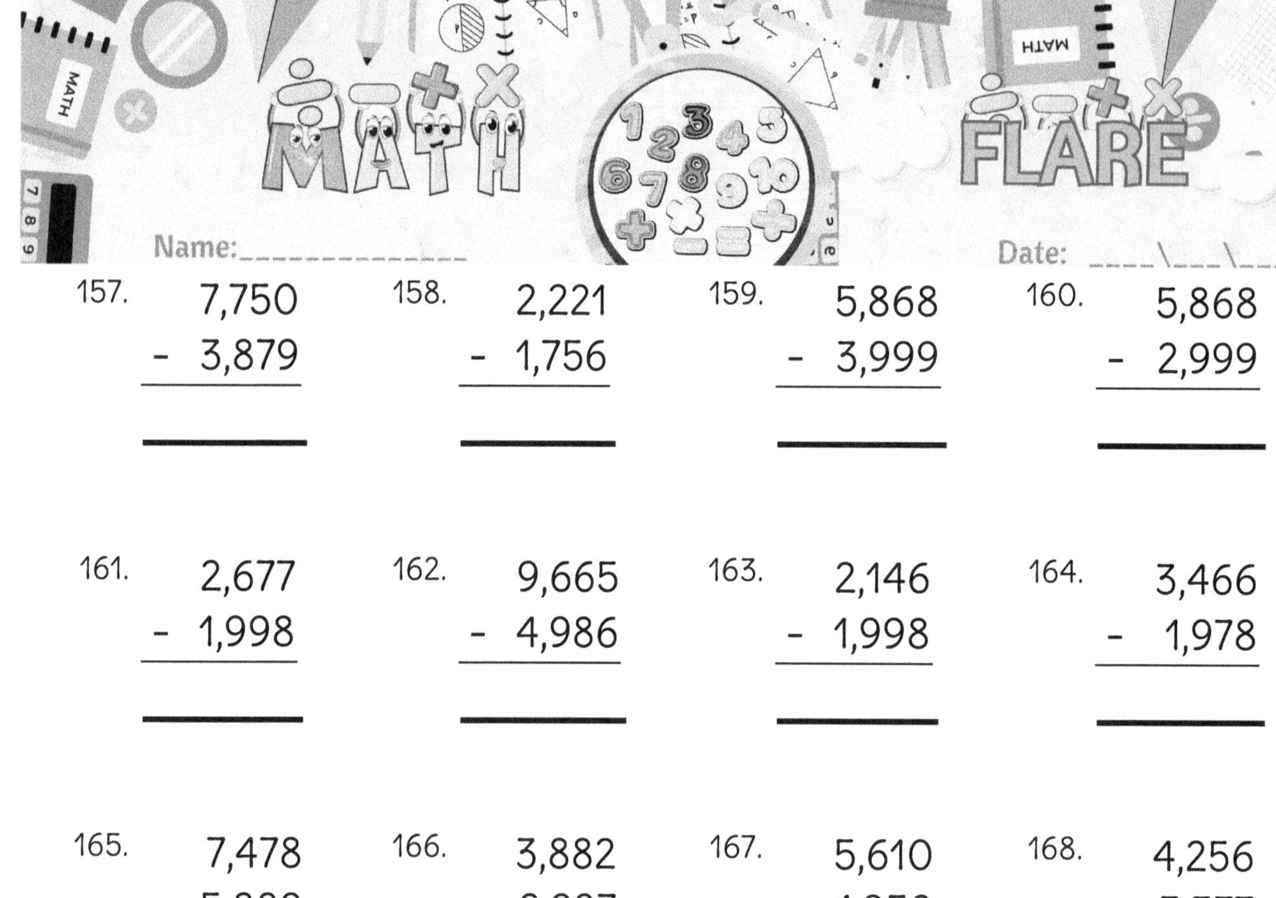

| | | | |
|---|---|---|---|
| 157.    7,750<br>   - 3,879 | 158.    2,221<br>   - 1,756 | 159.    5,868<br>   - 3,999 | 160.    5,868<br>   - 2,999 |
| 161.    2,677<br>   - 1,998 | 162.    9,665<br>   - 4,986 | 163.    2,146<br>   - 1,998 | 164.    3,466<br>   - 1,978 |
| 165.    7,478<br>   - 5,889 | 166.    3,882<br>   - 2,997 | 167.    5,610<br>   - 1,958 | 168.    4,256<br>   - 3,377 |
| 169.    9,644<br>   - 3,786 | 170.    2,026<br>   - 1,347 | 171.    8,882<br>   - 4,993 | 172.    2,756<br>   - 1,988 |
| 173.    2,301<br>   - 1,619 | 174.    3,288<br>   - 1,799 | 175.    9,743<br>   - 5,986 | 176.    2,681<br>   - 1,995 |

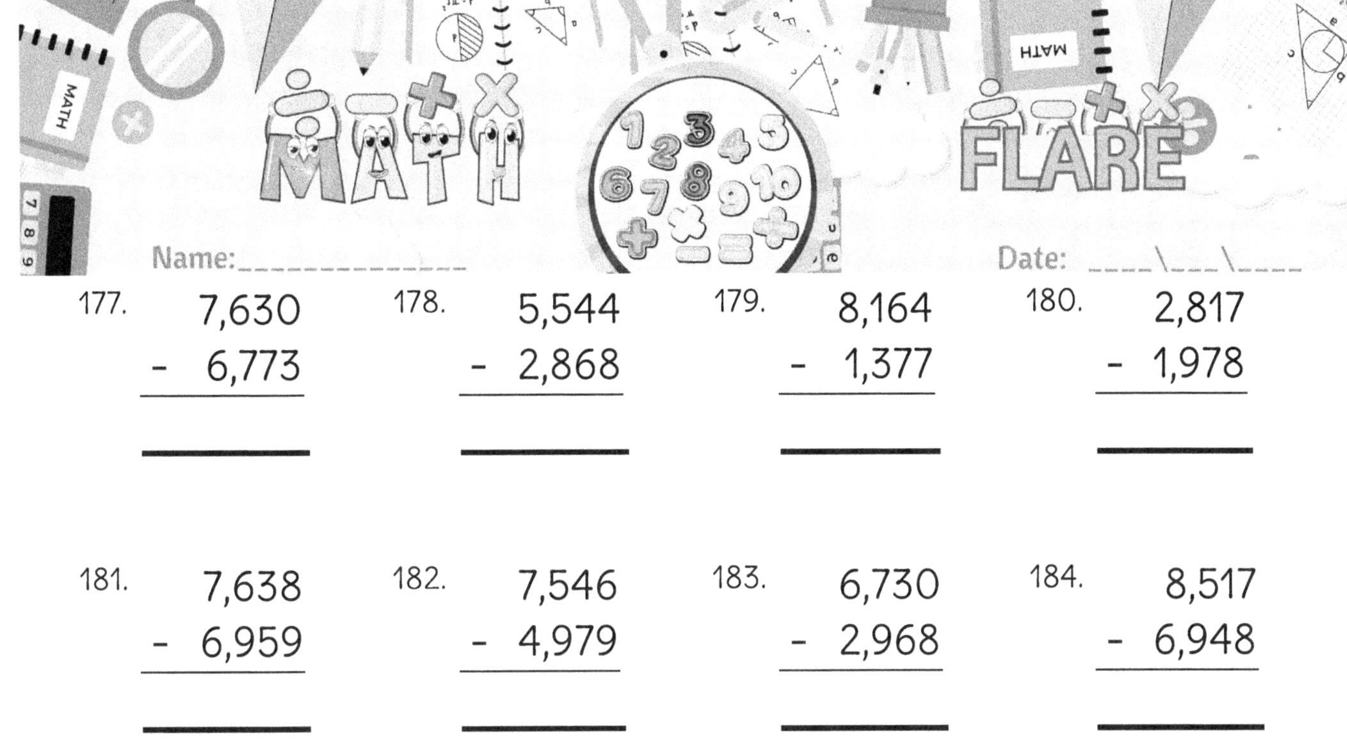



| | | | |
|---|---|---|---|
| 177.    7,630<br>− 6,773 | 178.    5,544<br>− 2,868 | 179.    8,164<br>− 1,377 | 180.    2,817<br>− 1,978 |
| 181.    7,638<br>− 6,959 | 182.    7,546<br>− 4,979 | 183.    6,730<br>− 2,968 | 184.    8,517<br>− 6,948 |
| 185.    2,516<br>− 1,958 | 186.    7,687<br>− 2,899 | 187.    5,163<br>− 4,696 | 188.    4,057<br>− 3,189 |
| 189.    5,326<br>− 4,947 | 190.    5,525<br>− 4,657 | 191.    5,572<br>− 4,784 | 192.    2,270<br>− 1,886 |
| 193.    6,288<br>− 3,899 | 194.    9,744<br>− 6,868 | 195.    6,568<br>− 5,979 | 196.    9,402<br>− 8,629 |

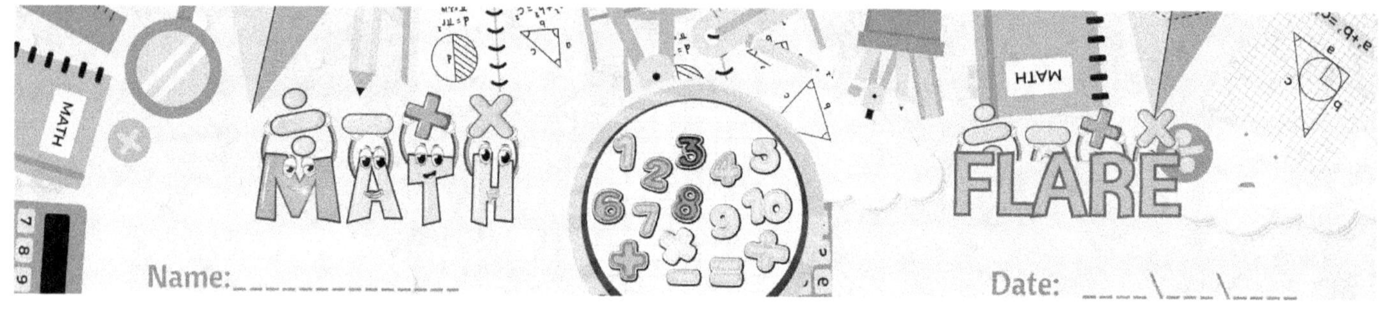


# Addition Unknown Number

Find the unknown number.

197.  272 + _______ = 1,210

198.  923 + _______ = 1,112

199.  789 + 642 = _______

200.  _______ + 848 = 1,320

201.  _______ + 895 = 1,210

202.  332 + _______ = 1,130

203.  775 + _______ = 1,620

204.  393 + 868 = _______

205.  572 + 839 = _______

206.  _______ + 894 = 1,830

207.  _______ + 537 = 1,231

208.  _______ + 899 = 1,610

209.  684 + _______ = 1,240

210.  912 + 298 = _______

211.  351 + 969 = _______

212.  317 + _______ = 1,213

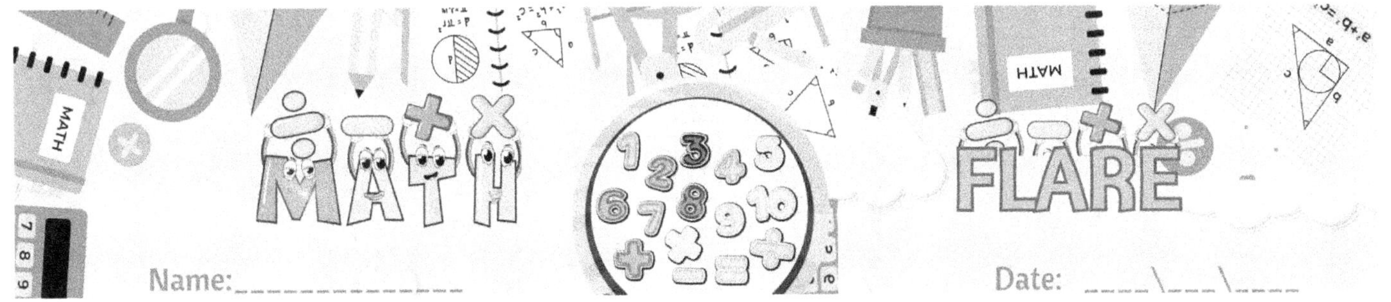


213. _______ + 895 = 1,320

214. 151 + 989 = _______

215. _______ + 379 = 1,353

216. 932 + 889 = _______

217. _______ + 678 = 1,227

218. 751 + 899 = _______

219. 731 + _______ = 1,330

220. 527 + _______ = 1,310

221. 186 + _______ = 1,183

222. 211 + 999 = _______

223. 118 + _______ = 1,113

224. 322 + _______ = 1,310

225. 321 + _______ = 1,320

226. _______ + 839 = 1,330

227. 739 + 478 = _______

228. 552 + 598 = _______

229. _______ + 776 = 1,134

230. 384 + 927 = _______

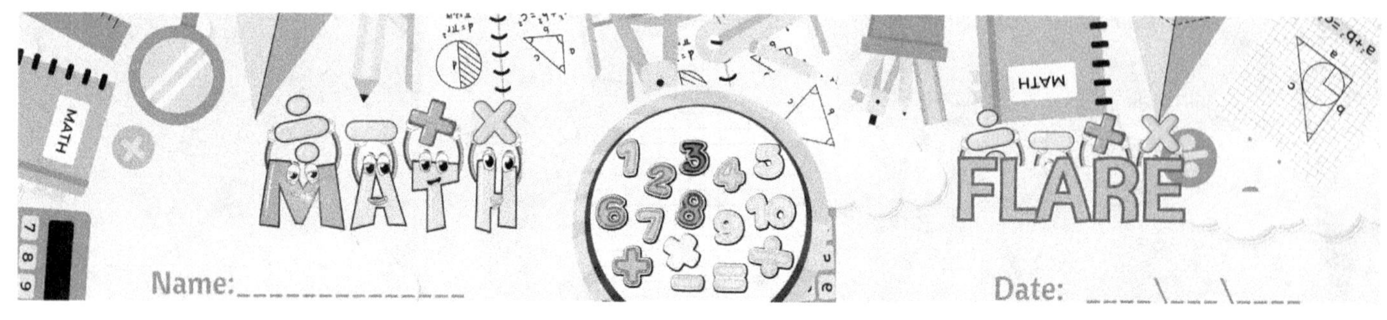


231. ______ + 849 = 1,644

232. 888 + ______ = 1,231

233. 897 + 647 = ______

234. ______ + 786 = 1,232

235. 483 + ______ = 1,332

236. 171 + 969 = ______

237. 125 + ______ = 1,114

238. 218 + ______ = 1,216

239. ______ + 988 = 1,147

240. 178 + ______ = 1,157

241. 631 + ______ = 1,420

242. 362 + 859 = ______

243. ______ + 695 = 1,533

244. 251 + 979 = ______

245. 195 + 917 = ______

246. ______ + 599 = 1,232

247. ______ + 896 = 1,130

248. ______ + 375 = 1,362

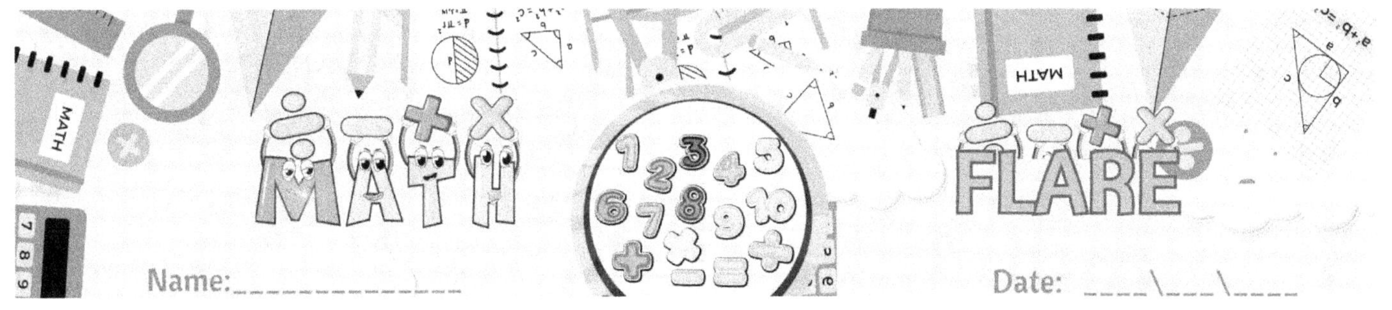


249. _______ + 889 = 1,210

250. 827 + _______ = 1,812

251. 698 + _______ = 1,374

252. 654 + _______ = 1,213

253. 151 + 959 = _______

254. _______ + 898 = 1,211

255. 171 + 939 = _______

256. 977 + _______ = 1,753

257. 158 + 964 = _______

258. 392 + 789 = _______

259. _______ + 766 = 1,313

260. 514 + 798 = _______

261. _______ + 676 = 1,572

262. _______ + 769 = 1,720

263. 286 + 877 = _______

264. 134 + _______ = 1,132

265. 231 + 879 = _______

266. 919 + _______ = 1,210

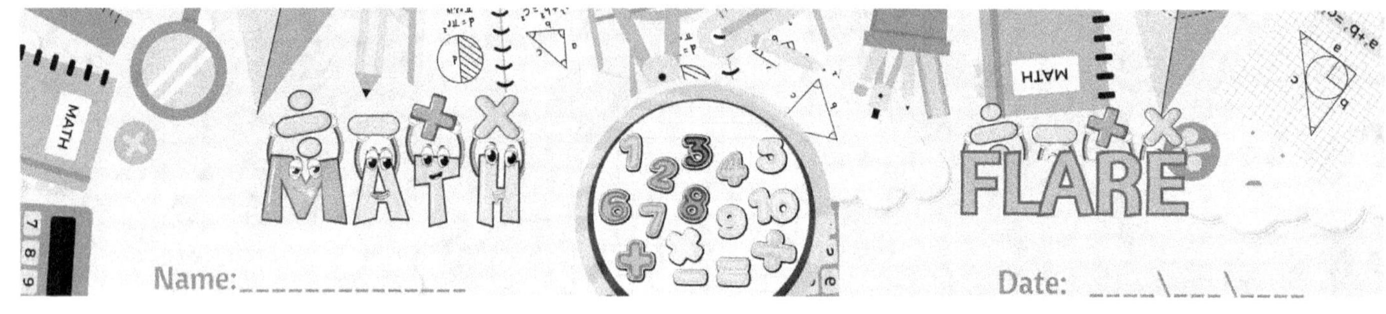


267. 752 + _____ = 1,151

268. _____ + 459 = 1,140

269. 458 + _____ = 1,322

270. _____ + 699 = 1,510

271. _____ + 638 = 1,120

272. 299 + 983 = _____

273. 736 + 886 = _____

274. _____ + 989 = 1,524

275. _____ + 799 = 1,110

276. 827 + _____ = 1,112

277. 463 + _____ = 1,140

278. 174 + 958 = _____

279. 325 + _____ = 1,210

280. 315 + _____ = 1,311

281. 291 + 999 = _____

282. 489 + 939 = _____

283. 492 + 789 = _____

284. 124 + _____ = 1,123

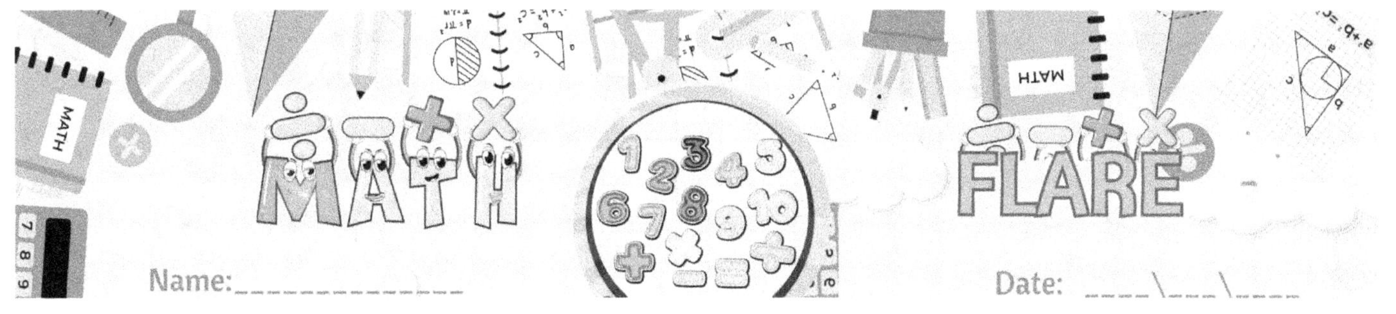


285. 423 + _____ = 1,411

286. 424 + _____ = 1,110

287. 335 + 889 = _____

288. 819 + 396 = _____

289. 875 + _____ = 1,142

290. _____ + 989 = 1,120

291. _____ + 968 = 1,110

292. 319 + 995 = _____

293. _____ + 998 = 1,112

294. _____ + 297 = 1,124

295. _____ + 997 = 1,130

296. _____ + 981 = 1,210

297. _____ + 667 = 1,313

298. 424 + 699 = _____

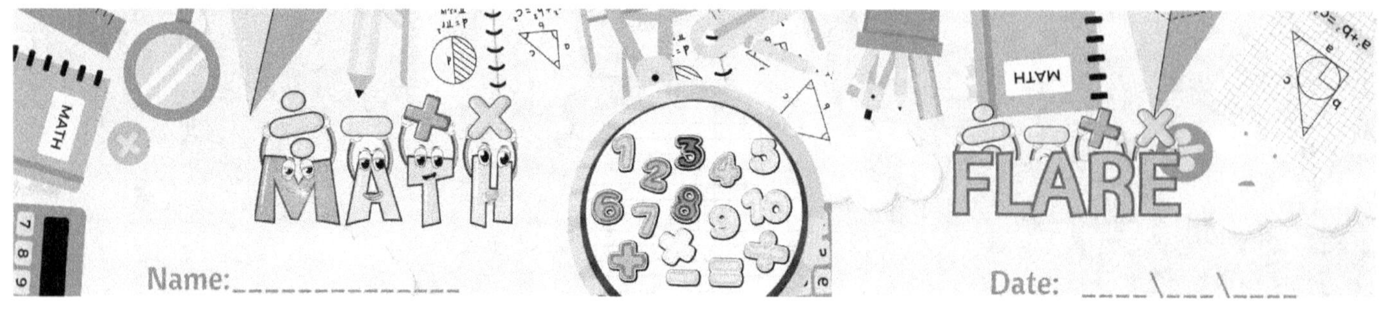

# Subtraction: Unknown Number

Find the unknown number.

299. _____ - 235 = 6

300. 391 - _____ = 16

301. 832 - _____ = 339

302. _____ - 314 = 491

303. 880 - _____ = 658

304. 949 - 547 = _____

305. 805 - _____ = 151

306. 746 - 142 = _____

307. 854 - 758 = _____

308. 531 - 237 = _____

309. _____ - 348 = 234

310. _____ - 272 = 63

311. 958 - 860 = _____

312. _____ - 342 = 575

313. 809 - _____ = 116

314. 141 - 100 = _____

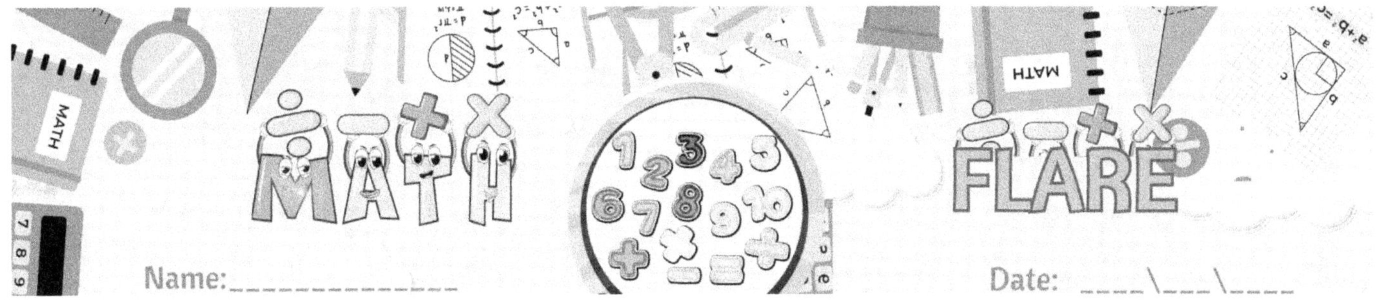


315. 564 - 167 = _____

316. 226 - _____ = 12

317. 875 - _____ = 705

318. _____ - 353 = 243

319. _____ - 192 = 7

320. _____ - 138 = 7

321. 784 - _____ = 490

322. 421 - 181 = _____

323. 410 - _____ = 285

324. 716 - _____ = 164

325. 795 - 130 = _____

326. 208 - _____ = 39

327. 725 - _____ = 254

328. 991 - _____ = 64

329. 665 - 376 = _____

330. 563 - 114 = _____

331. _____ - 193 = 7

332. 109 - 106 = _____

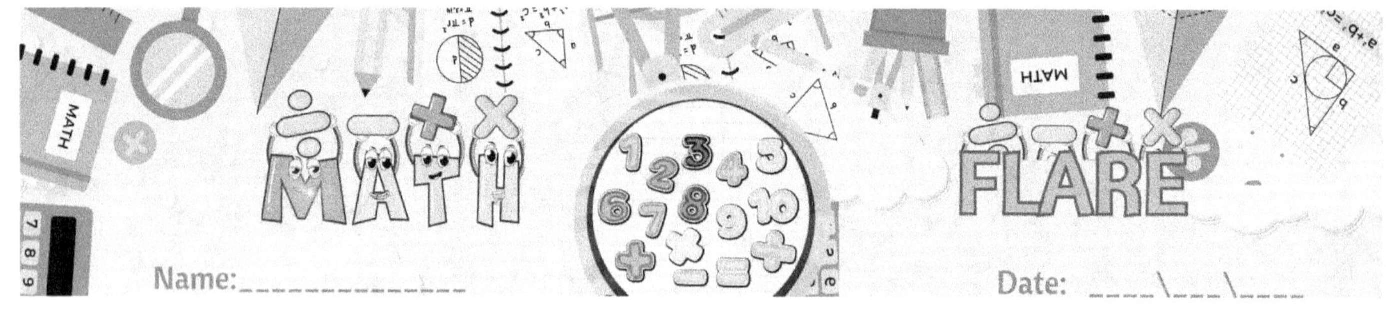


333. 681 - _____ = 109

334. _____ - 236 = 46

335. 389 - 380 = _____

336. 287 - 213 = _____

337. _____ - 272 = 245

338. 972 - 685 = _____

339. _____ - 413 = 162

340. 955 - _____ = 249

341. 236 - 142 = _____

342. _____ - 201 = 112

343. 121 - _____ = 11

344. _____ - 151 = 139

345. _____ - 156 = 34

346. _____ - 592 = 300

347. 473 - _____ = 366

348. 762 - _____ = 115

349. 346 - _____ = 70

350. 644 - 389 = _____

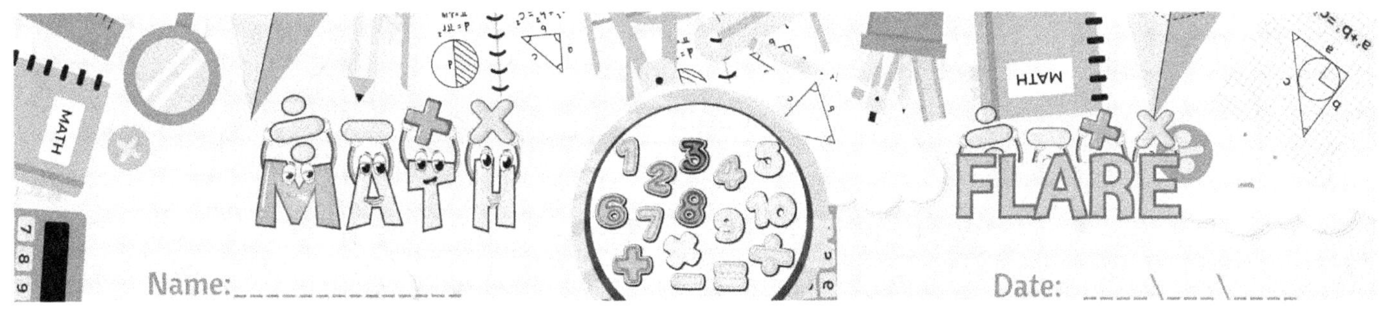


351.  888 - _____ = 49

352.  471 - 398 = _____

353.  851 - 486 = _____

354.  _____ - 145 = 115

355.  660 - 279 = _____

356.  460 - 449 = _____

357.  583 - _____ = 94

358.  _____ - 733 = 158

359.  _____ - 437 = 291

360.  _____ - 182 = 473

361.  641 - _____ = 36

362.  _____ - 507 = 176

363.  180 - 147 = _____

364.  272 - _____ = 96

365.  709 - 187 = _____

366.  _____ - 391 = 67

367.  148 - _____ = 28

368.  _____ - 260 = 588

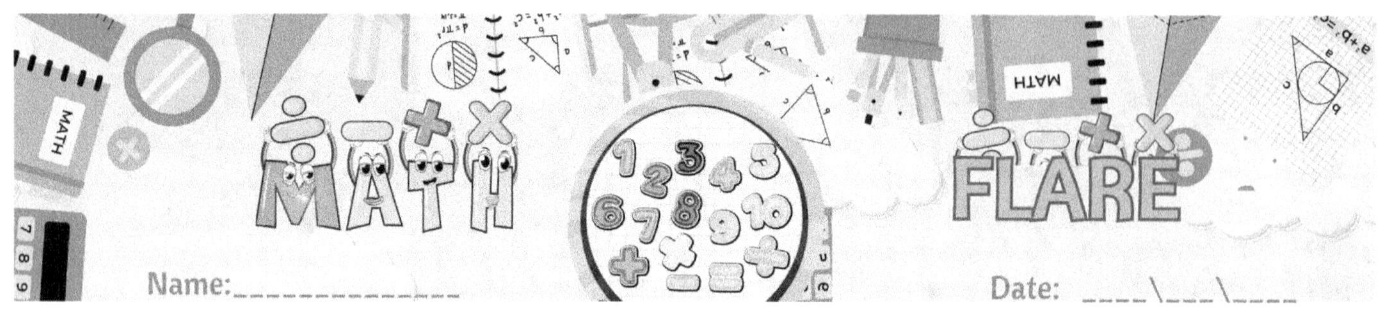


369. _____ - 451 = 457

370. 673 - 392 = _____

371. 388 - _____ = 20

372. 680 - 553 = _____

373. _____ - 282 = 18

374. 175 - _____ = 29

375. _____ - 218 = 8

376. 215 - _____ = 30

377. _____ - 141 = 48

378. _____ - 889 = 47

379. _____ - 286 = 74

380. 741 - 260 = _____

381. _____ - 313 = 77

382. 644 - 361 = _____

383. _____ - 588 = 341

384. 924 - 198 = _____

385. _____ - 683 = 292

386. _____ - 314 = 597

387. _____ - 188 = 721

388. 844 - _____ = 244

389. 359 - _____ = 34

390. _____ - 176 = 351

391. _____ - 363 = 189

392. 374 - 303 = _____

393. 114 - _____ = 5

394. _____ - 482 = 259

395. _____ - 490 = 49

396. 931 - 252 = _____

397. _____ - 352 = 397

398. _____ - 199 = 69

399. _____ - 148 = 243

400. _____ - 589 = 283

401. 994 - _____ = 32

402. _____ - 370 = 301

403. 131 - _____ = 4

404. 852 - _____ = 8

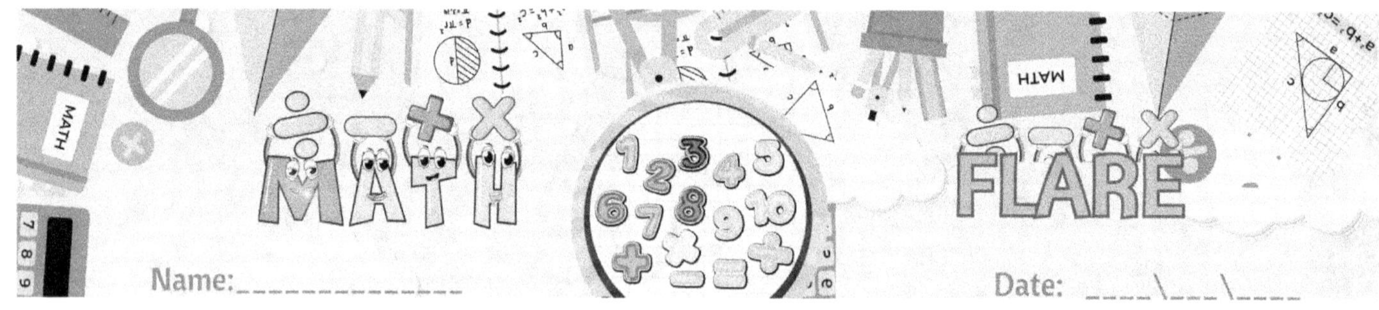



# Addition (3 Addends)

Find the sum.

| 405. | 406. | 407. | 408. |
|---|---|---|---|
| 7,738 | 3,414 | 9,830 | 6,446 |
| 5,482 | 7,848 | 3,701 | 6,994 |
| + 2,176 | + 5,261 | + 8,295 | + 6,826 |

| 409. | 410. | 411. | 412. |
|---|---|---|---|
| 1,226 | 1,970 | 3,888 | 4,443 |
| 9,612 | 3,089 | 4,189 | 6,251 |
| + 7,306 | + 2,450 | + 9,123 | + 2,428 |

| 413. | 414. | 415. | 416. |
|---|---|---|---|
| 3,703 | 8,279 | 5,821 | 8,458 |
| 2,444 | 7,012 | 1,104 | 4,347 |
| + 5,791 | + 9,502 | + 8,452 | + 5,794 |

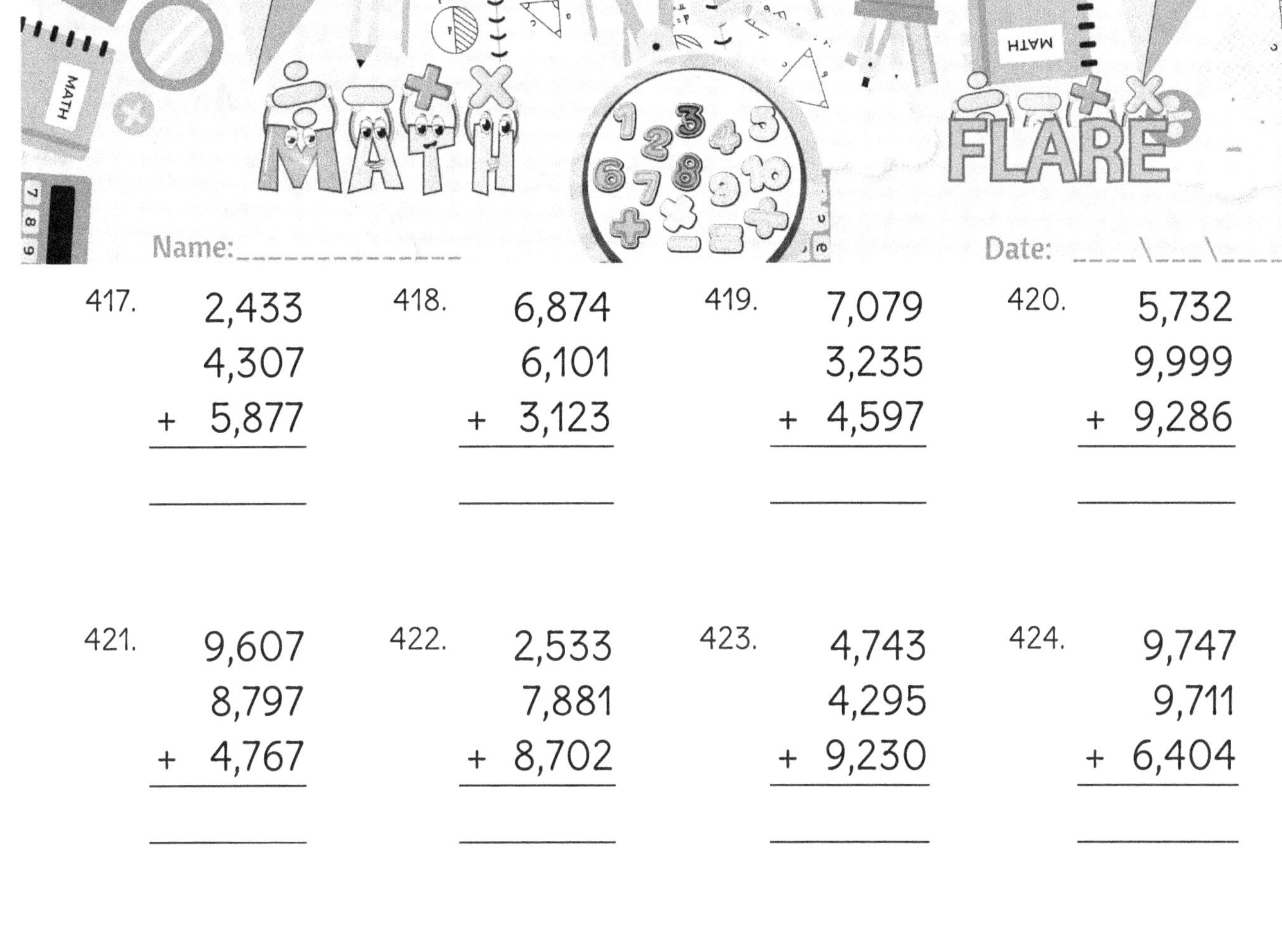



417.    2,433
      4,307
+ 5,877

418.    6,874
      6,101
+ 3,123

419.    7,079
      3,235
+ 4,597

420.    5,732
      9,999
+ 9,286

421.    9,607
      8,797
+ 4,767

422.    2,533
      7,881
+ 8,702

423.    4,743
      4,295
+ 9,230

424.    9,747
      9,711
+ 6,404

425.    9,468
      2,552
+ 6,688

426.    8,792
      1,626
+ 6,890

427.    8,373
      2,767
+ 6,265

428.    2,513
      9,536
+ 8,781

429.    6,572
      7,013
+ 8,087

430.    7,000
      7,363
+ 4,016

431.    7,830
      7,970
+ 2,444

432.    6,505
      8,671
+ 8,214

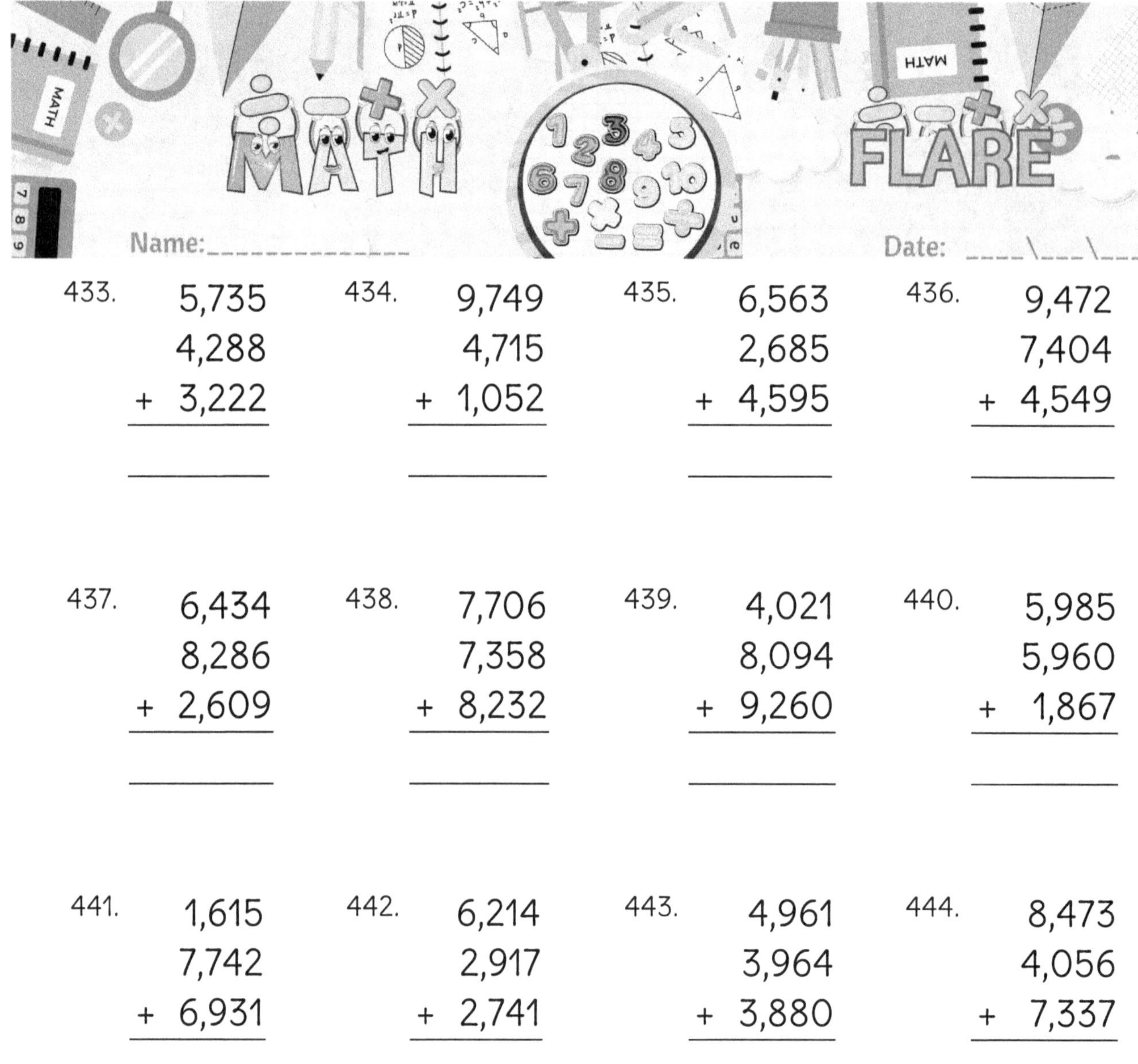



| | | | |
|---|---|---|---|
| 433.  5,735<br>4,288<br>+ 3,222 | 434.  9,749<br>4,715<br>+ 1,052 | 435.  6,563<br>2,685<br>+ 4,595 | 436.  9,472<br>7,404<br>+ 4,549 |
| 437.  6,434<br>8,286<br>+ 2,609 | 438.  7,706<br>7,358<br>+ 8,232 | 439.  4,021<br>8,094<br>+ 9,260 | 440.  5,985<br>5,960<br>+ 1,867 |
| 441.  1,615<br>7,742<br>+ 6,931 | 442.  6,214<br>2,917<br>+ 2,741 | 443.  4,961<br>3,964<br>+ 3,880 | 444.  8,473<br>4,056<br>+ 7,337 |
| 445.  4,668<br>8,623<br>+ 8,050 | 446.  6,212<br>5,949<br>+ 7,851 | 447.  5,186<br>7,100<br>+ 9,608 | 448.  4,537<br>1,566<br>+ 9,076 |

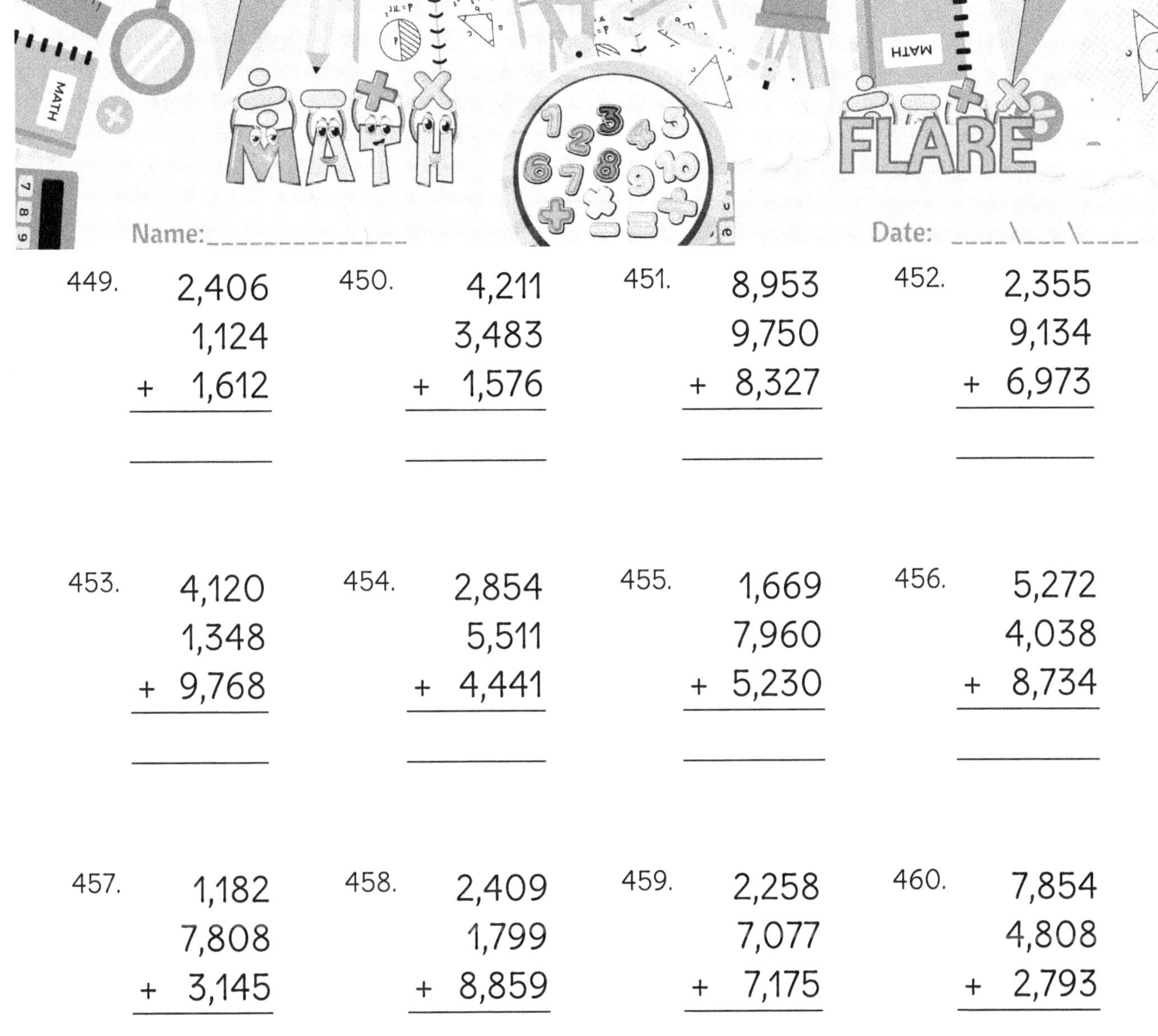

| | | | |
|---|---|---|---|
| 449.  2,406<br>1,124<br>+ 1,612 | 450.  4,211<br>3,483<br>+ 1,576 | 451.  8,953<br>9,750<br>+ 8,327 | 452.  2,355<br>9,134<br>+ 6,973 |
| 453.  4,120<br>1,348<br>+ 9,768 | 454.  2,854<br>5,511<br>+ 4,441 | 455.  1,669<br>7,960<br>+ 5,230 | 456.  5,272<br>4,038<br>+ 8,734 |
| 457.  1,182<br>7,808<br>+ 3,145 | 458.  2,409<br>1,799<br>+ 8,859 | 459.  2,258<br>7,077<br>+ 7,175 | 460.  7,854<br>4,808<br>+ 2,793 |
| 461.  2,129<br>1,750<br>+ 1,480 | 462.  3,304<br>9,519<br>+ 4,306 | 463.  9,009<br>3,314<br>+ 9,488 | 464.  2,078<br>3,092<br>+ 5,601 |

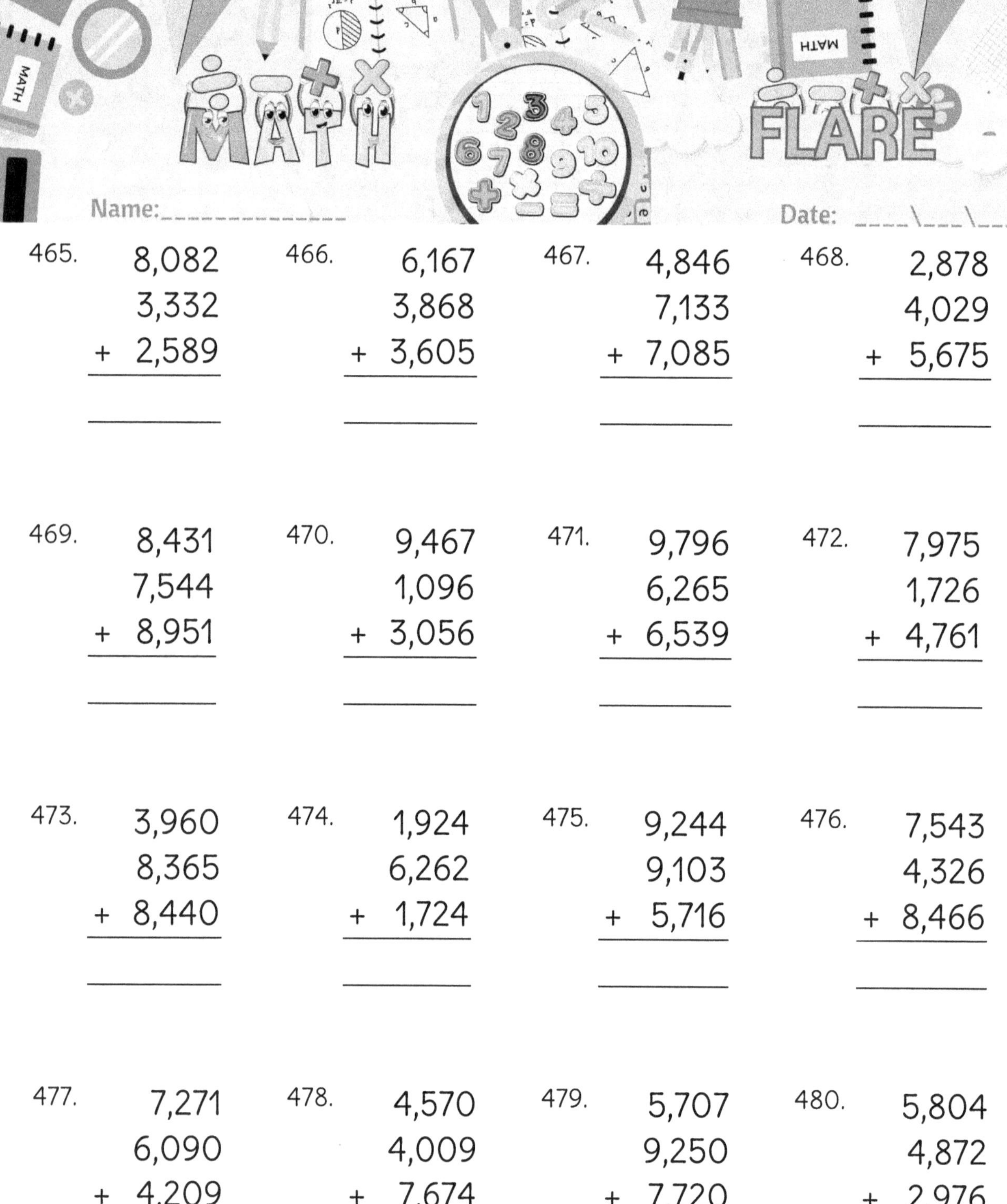



| | | | |
|---|---|---|---|
| 465.     8,082<br>3,332<br>+ 2,589 | 466.     6,167<br>3,868<br>+ 3,605 | 467.     4,846<br>7,133<br>+ 7,085 | 468.     2,878<br>4,029<br>+ 5,675 |
| 469.     8,431<br>7,544<br>+ 8,951 | 470.     9,467<br>1,096<br>+ 3,056 | 471.     9,796<br>6,265<br>+ 6,539 | 472.     7,975<br>1,726<br>+ 4,761 |
| 473.     3,960<br>8,365<br>+ 8,440 | 474.     1,924<br>6,262<br>+ 1,724 | 475.     9,244<br>9,103<br>+ 5,716 | 476.     7,543<br>4,326<br>+ 8,466 |
| 477.     7,271<br>6,090<br>+ 4,209 | 478.     4,570<br>4,009<br>+ 7,674 | 479.     5,707<br>9,250<br>+ 7,720 | 480.     5,804<br>4,872<br>+ 2,976 |

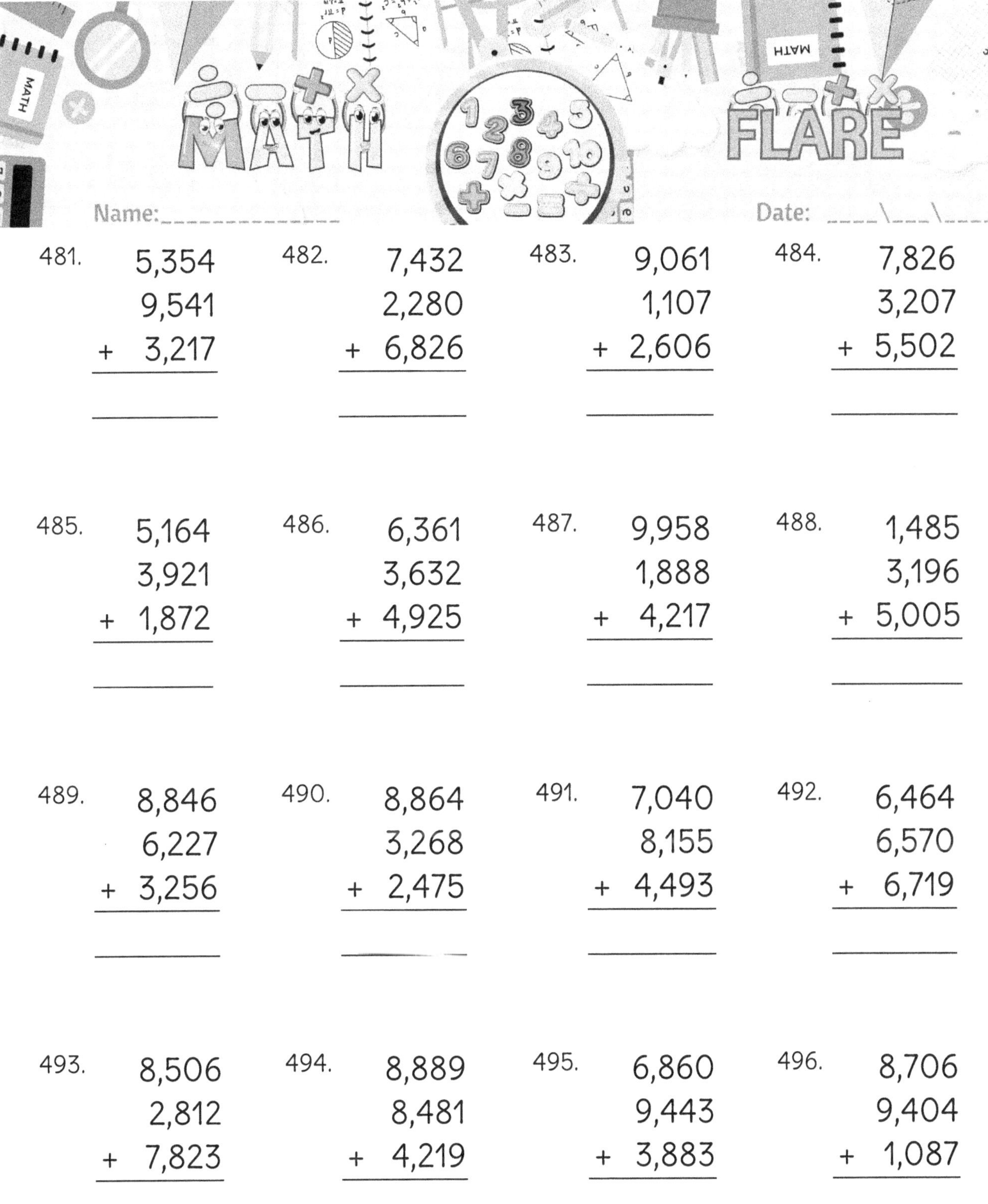

Name:____________________  Date: ______________

| | | | |
|---|---|---|---|
| 481.    5,354<br>9,541<br>+ 3,217 | 482.    7,432<br>2,280<br>+ 6,826 | 483.    9,061<br>1,107<br>+ 2,606 | 484.    7,826<br>3,207<br>+ 5,502 |
| 485.    5,164<br>3,921<br>+ 1,872 | 486.    6,361<br>3,632<br>+ 4,925 | 487.    9,958<br>1,888<br>+ 4,217 | 488.    1,485<br>3,196<br>+ 5,005 |
| 489.    8,846<br>6,227<br>+ 3,256 | 490.    8,864<br>3,268<br>+ 2,475 | 491.    7,040<br>8,155<br>+ 4,493 | 492.    6,464<br>6,570<br>+ 6,719 |
| 493.    8,506<br>2,812<br>+ 7,823 | 494.    8,889<br>8,481<br>+ 4,219 | 495.    6,860<br>9,443<br>+ 3,883 | 496.    8,706<br>9,404<br>+ 1,087 |

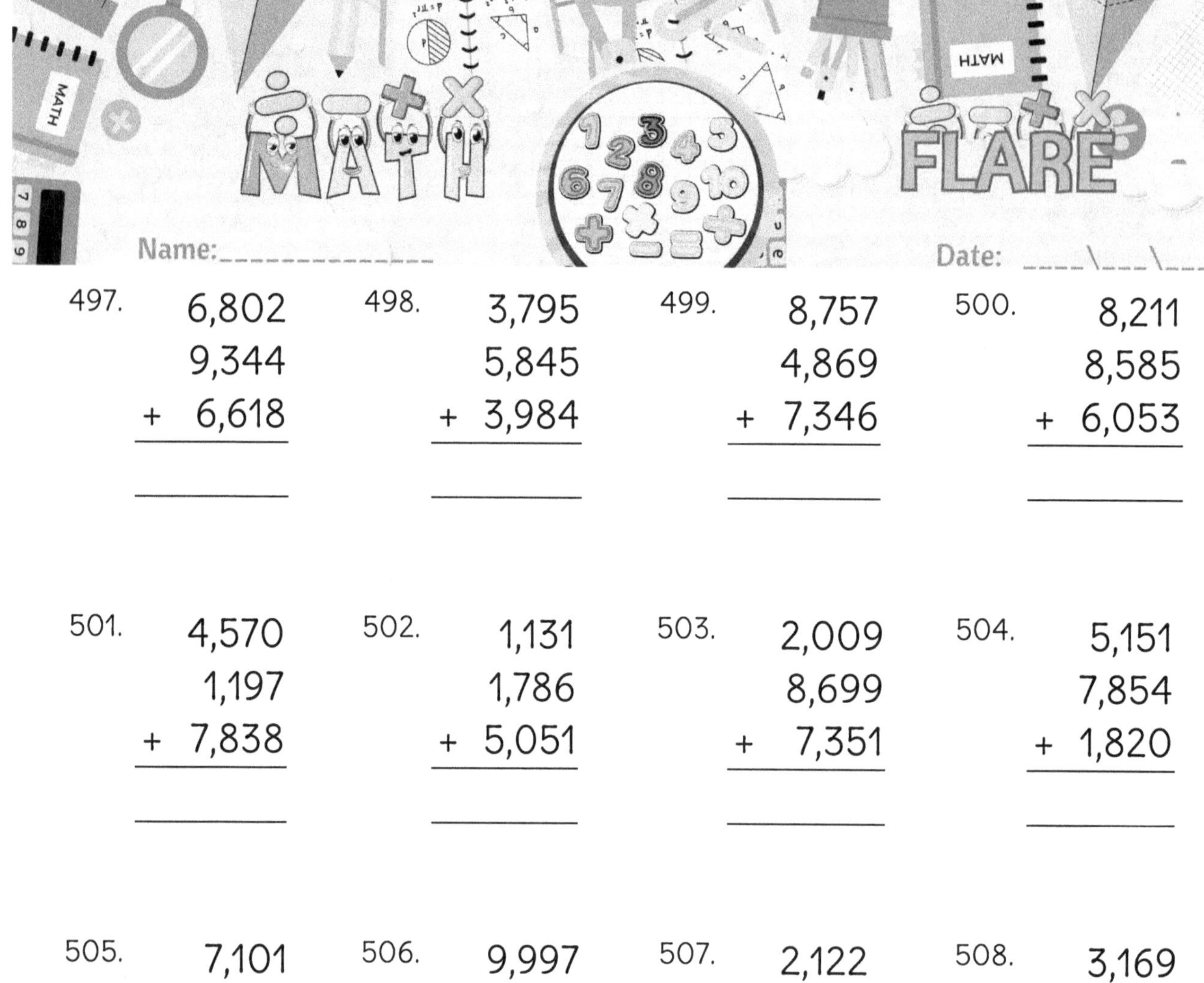

| 497. | 498. | 499. | 500. |
|---|---|---|---|
| 6,802<br>9,344<br>+ 6,618 | 3,795<br>5,845<br>+ 3,984 | 8,757<br>4,869<br>+ 7,346 | 8,211<br>8,585<br>+ 6,053 |
| 501. | 502. | 503. | 504. |
| 4,570<br>1,197<br>+ 7,838 | 1,131<br>1,786<br>+ 5,051 | 2,009<br>8,699<br>+ 7,351 | 5,151<br>7,854<br>+ 1,820 |
| 505. | 506. | 507. | 508. |
| 7,101<br>2,070<br>+ 3,406 | 9,997<br>4,624<br>+ 3,751 | 2,122<br>1,140<br>+ 6,821 | 3,169<br>3,062<br>+ 3,923 |
| 509. | 510. | 511. | 512. |
| 5,856<br>4,245<br>+ 3,310 | 1,508<br>7,706<br>+ 2,701 | 9,373<br>1,295<br>+ 4,227 | 2,770<br>5,319<br>+ 8,284 |

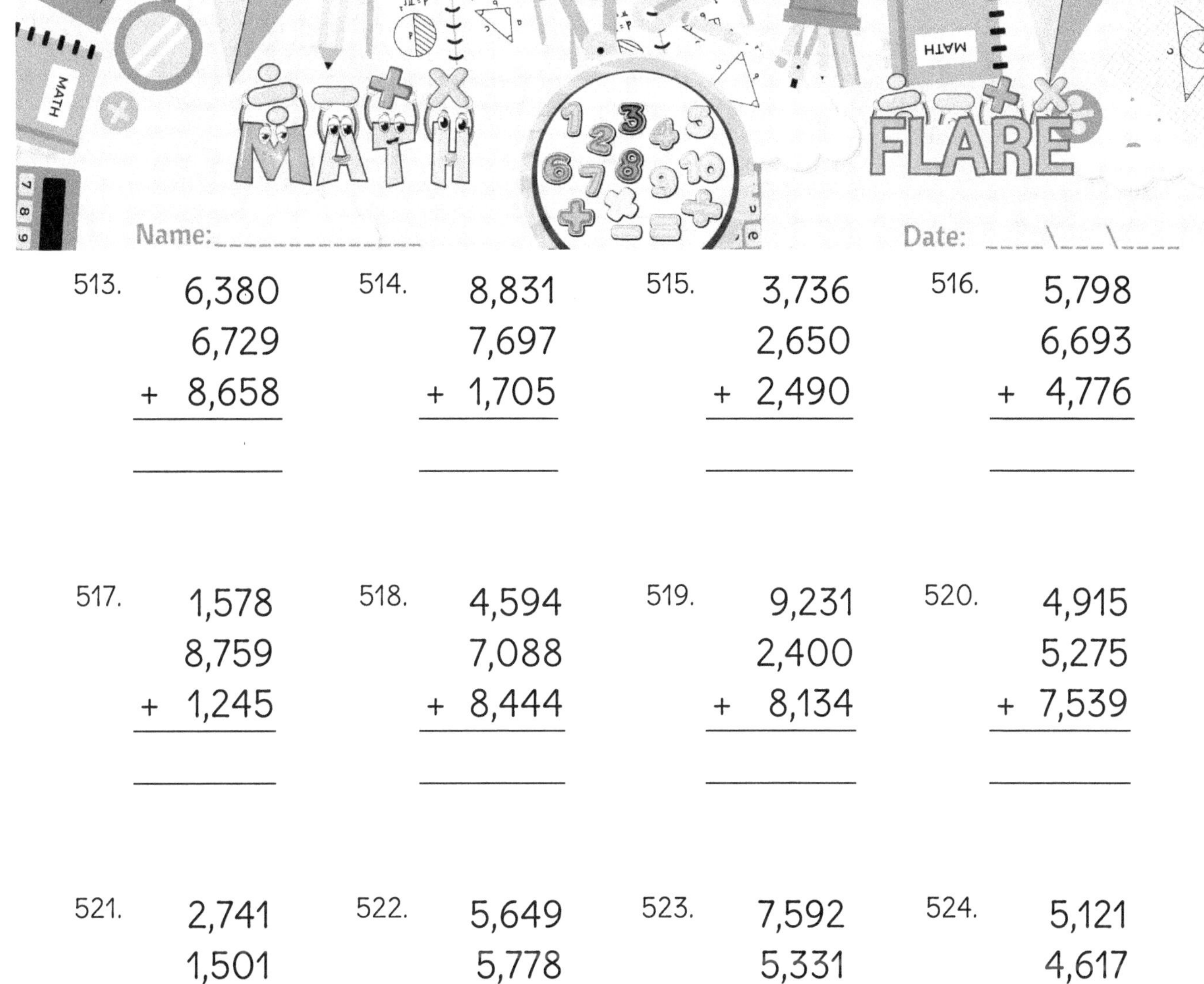



Name:_________________ Date: _______________

| | | | |
|---|---|---|---|
| 513.  6,380<br>6,729<br>+ 8,658 | 514.  8,831<br>7,697<br>+ 1,705 | 515.  3,736<br>2,650<br>+ 2,490 | 516.  5,798<br>6,693<br>+ 4,776 |
| 517.  1,578<br>8,759<br>+ 1,245 | 518.  4,594<br>7,088<br>+ 8,444 | 519.  9,231<br>2,400<br>+ 8,134 | 520.  4,915<br>5,275<br>+ 7,539 |
| 521.  2,741<br>1,501<br>+ 1,993 | 522.  5,649<br>5,778<br>+ 7,560 | 523.  7,592<br>5,331<br>+ 6,749 | 524.  5,121<br>4,617<br>+ 7,894 |
| 525.  5,093<br>3,290<br>+ 3,443 | 526.  6,116<br>9,432<br>+ 1,412 | 527.  2,433<br>1,058<br>+ 7,552 | 528.  8,533<br>9,929<br>+ 8,946 |

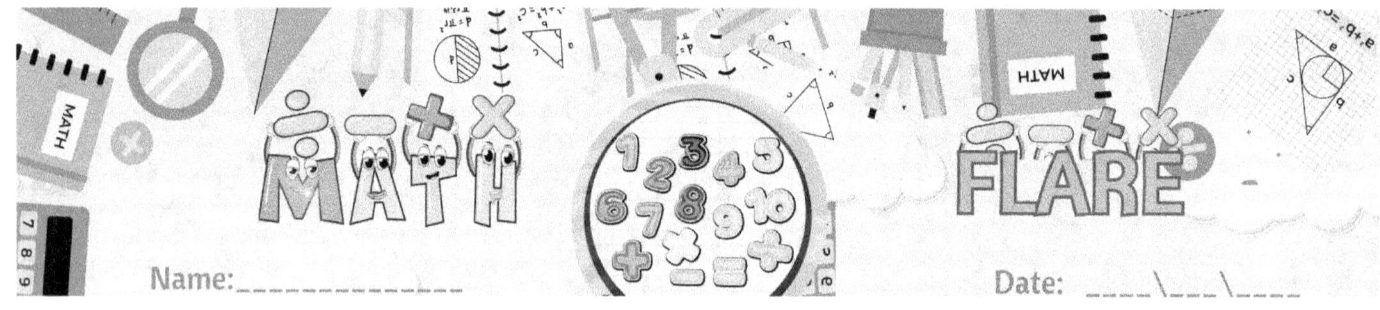

# Multiple Operations: Addition Subtraction

Find the sum.

| 529. | 7,760<br>3,180<br>−  1,116<br>−  2,395 | 530. | 6,032<br>−  2,217<br>−  2,280<br>2,144 | 531. | 9,196<br>−  4,414<br>−  3,681<br>7,214 |
|---|---|---|---|---|---|
| 532. | 8,941<br>−  5,024<br>6,897<br>−  1,537 | 533. | 7,374<br>5,802<br>−  2,360<br>−  1,309 | 534. | 8,925<br>8,477<br>−  4,641<br>−  3,647 |
| 535. | 5,896<br>1,196<br>−  4,873<br>−  1,203 | 536. | 6,576<br>−  1,226<br>−  3,438<br>5,160 | 537. | 7,721<br>−  2,756<br>4,311<br>−  4,684 |
| 538. | 6,851<br>4,538<br>−  4,122<br>−  5,448 | 539. | 9,925<br>5,855<br>−  2,686<br>−  4,347 | 540. | 9,553<br>9,072<br>−  1,446<br>−  2,537 |

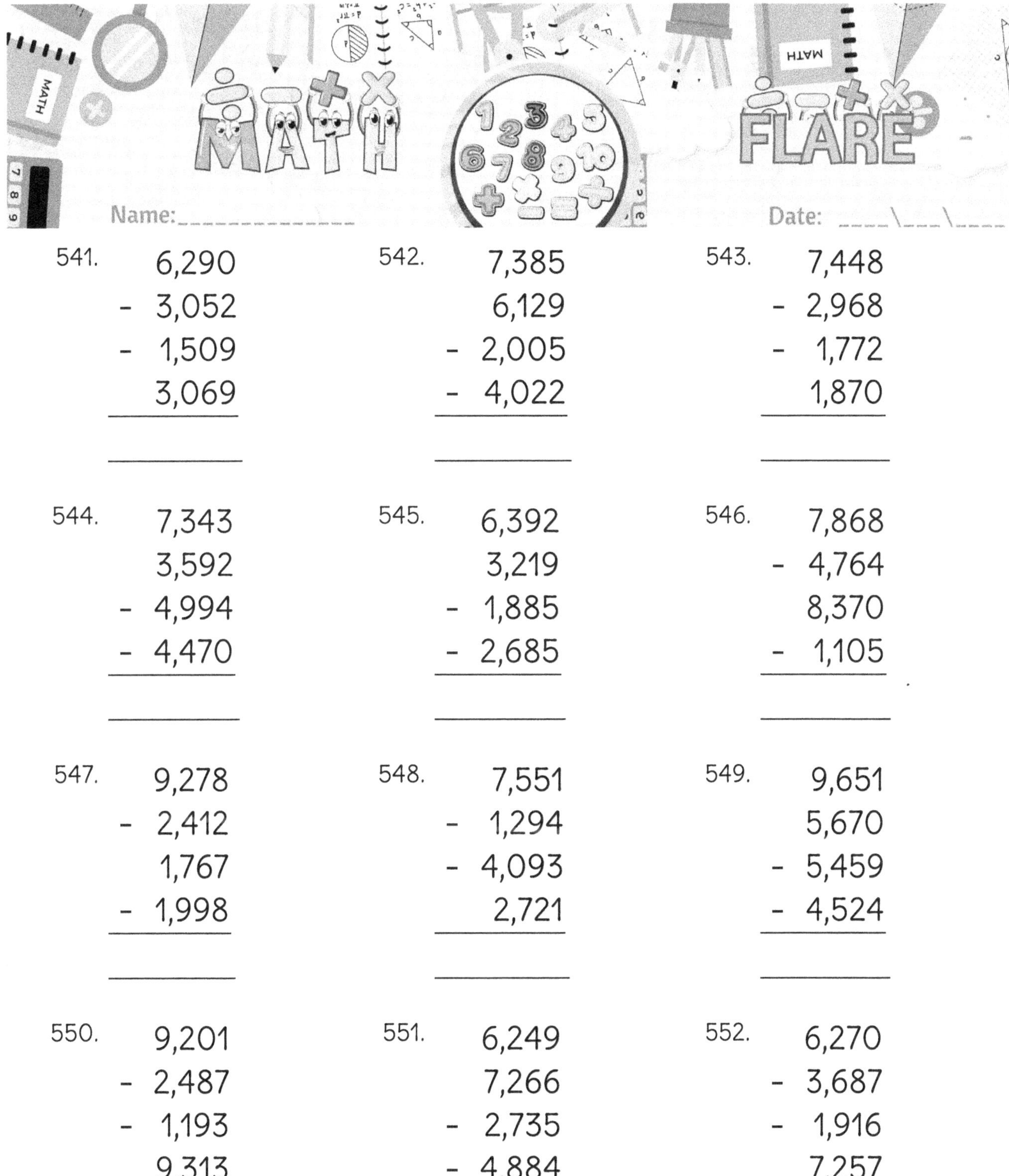

| 541. | 6,290<br>- 3,052<br>- 1,509<br>3,069 | 542. | 7,385<br>6,129<br>- 2,005<br>- 4,022 | 543. | 7,448<br>- 2,968<br>- 1,772<br>1,870 |
| --- | --- | --- | --- | --- | --- |
| 544. | 7,343<br>3,592<br>- 4,994<br>- 4,470 | 545. | 6,392<br>3,219<br>- 1,885<br>- 2,685 | 546. | 7,868<br>- 4,764<br>8,370<br>- 1,105 |
| 547. | 9,278<br>- 2,412<br>1,767<br>- 1,998 | 548. | 7,551<br>- 1,294<br>- 4,093<br>2,721 | 549. | 9,651<br>5,670<br>- 5,459<br>- 4,524 |
| 550. | 9,201<br>- 2,487<br>- 1,193<br>9,313 | 551. | 6,249<br>7,266<br>- 2,735<br>- 4,884 | 552. | 6,270<br>- 3,687<br>- 1,916<br>7,257 |

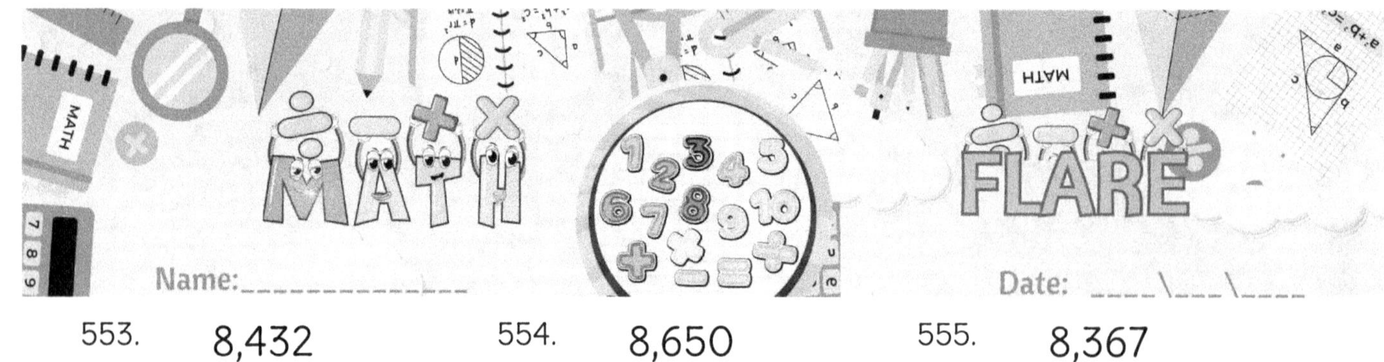



| | | |
|---|---|---|
| 553.    8,432<br>−   3,715<br>−   3,027<br>    6,888<br>———— | 554.    8,650<br>    7,523<br>−   4,669<br>−   2,526<br>———— | 555.    8,367<br>−   1,918<br>−   2,755<br>    1,947<br>———— |
| 556.    7,680<br>    1,015<br>−   1,969<br>−   2,654<br>———— | 557.    8,874<br>    1,274<br>−   1,783<br>−   5,009<br>———— | 558.    6,836<br>−   1,470<br>    9,538<br>−   4,905<br>———— |
| 559.    6,414<br>    3,456<br>−   1,934<br>−   4,735<br>———— | 560.    7,528<br>−   5,301<br>−   2,046<br>    3,182<br>———— | 561.    8,808<br>−   2,755<br>−   3,565<br>    8,673<br>———— |
| 562.    7,839<br>    1,299<br>−   3,209<br>−   1,889<br>———— | 563.    8,666<br>    6,865<br>−   1,656<br>−   3,782<br>———— | 564.    9,731<br>    9,439<br>−   2,976<br>−   1,742<br>———— |

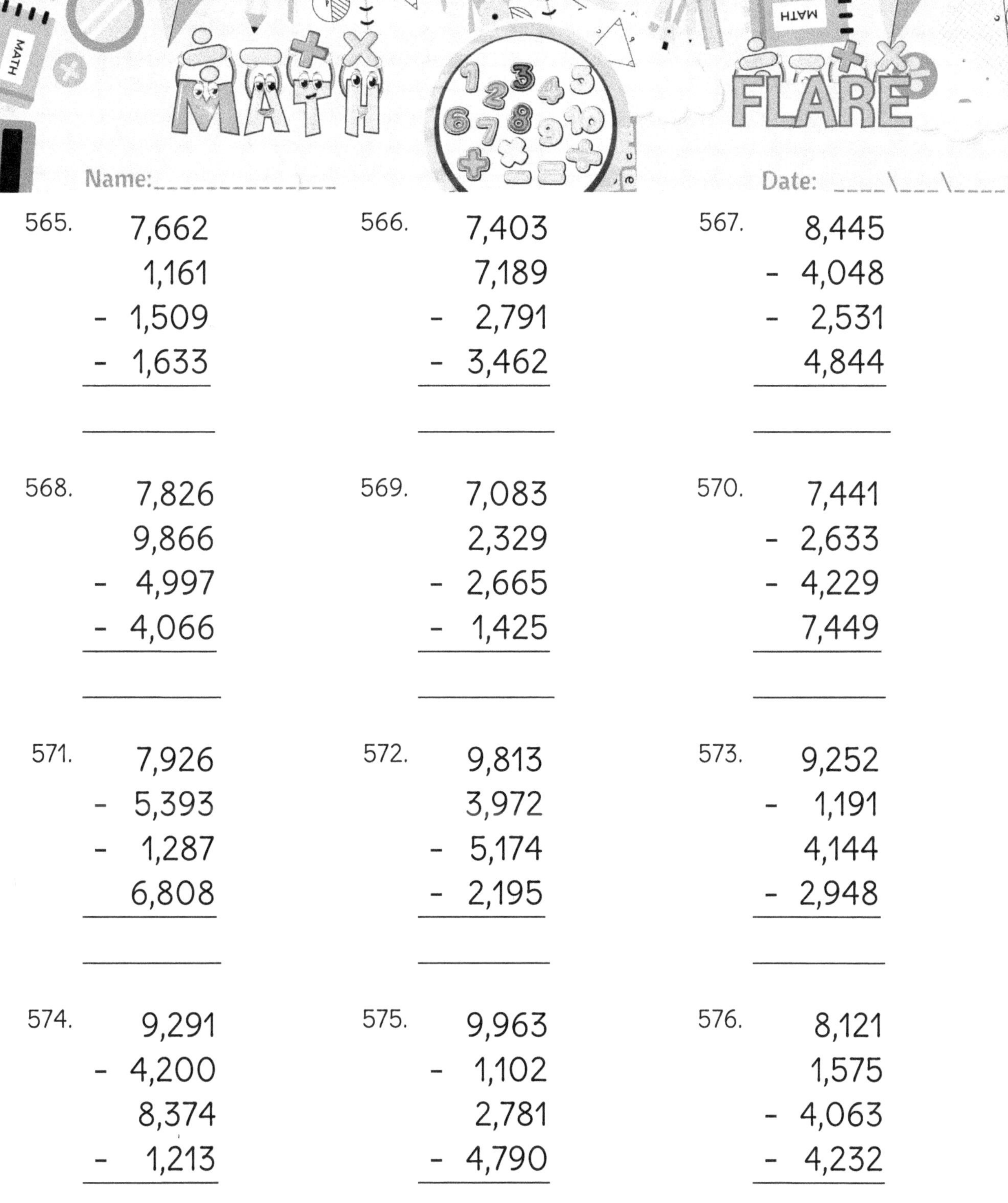

565.
```
    7,662
    1,161
  - 1,509
  - 1,633
  _______
```

566.
```
    7,403
    7,189
  - 2,791
  - 3,462
  _______
```

567.
```
    8,445
  - 4,048
  - 2,531
    4,844
  _______
```

568.
```
    7,826
    9,866
  - 4,997
  - 4,066
  _______
```

569.
```
    7,083
    2,329
  - 2,665
  - 1,425
  _______
```

570.
```
    7,441
  - 2,633
  - 4,229
    7,449
  _______
```

571.
```
    7,926
  - 5,393
  - 1,287
    6,808
  _______
```

572.
```
    9,813
    3,972
  - 5,174
  - 2,195
  _______
```

573.
```
    9,252
  - 1,191
    4,144
  - 2,948
  _______
```

574.
```
    9,291
  - 4,200
    8,374
  - 1,213
  _______
```

575.
```
    9,963
  - 1,102
    2,781
  - 4,790
  _______
```

576.
```
    8,121
    1,575
  - 4,063
  - 4,232
  _______
```

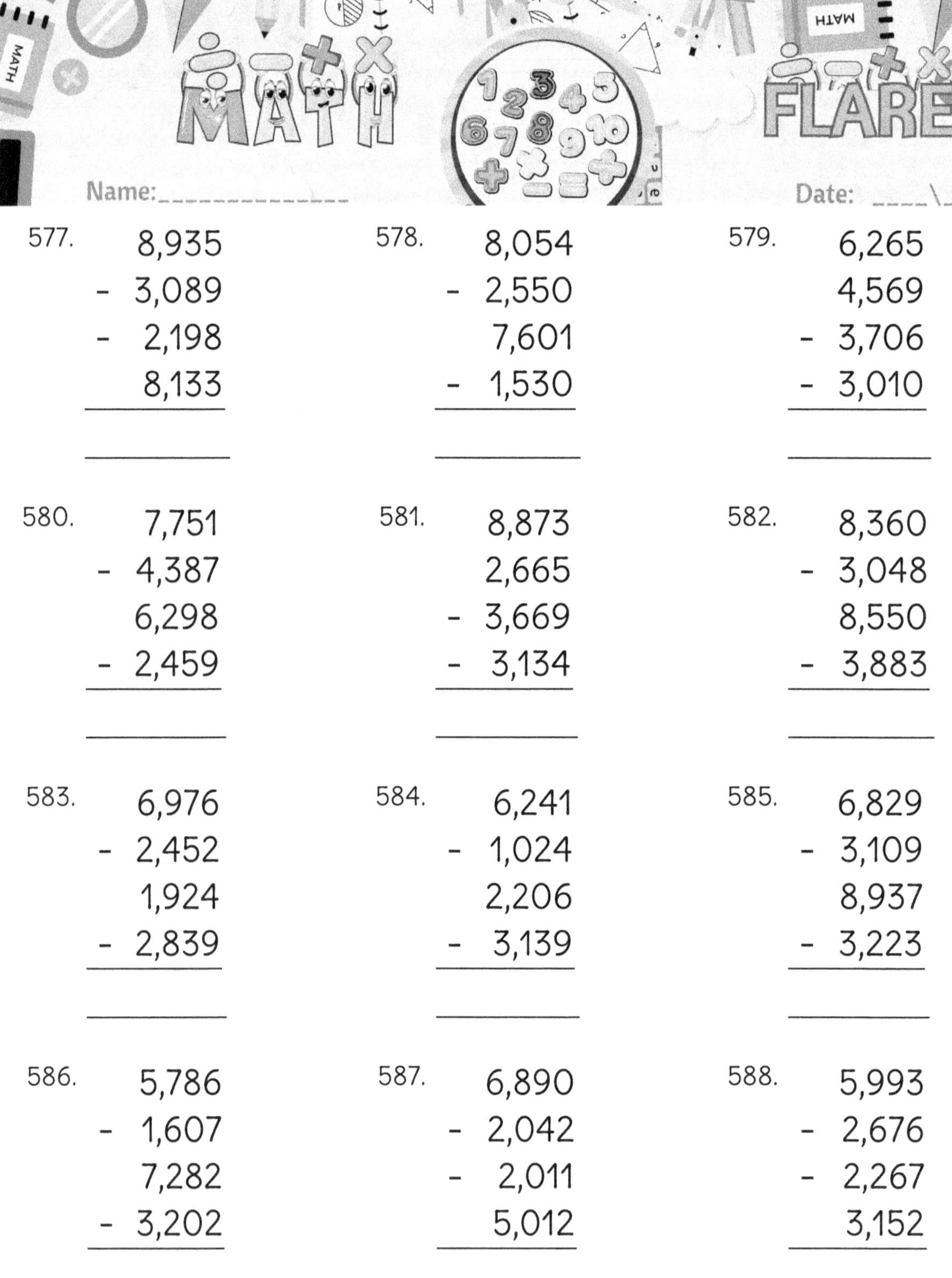

577.
```
    8,935
  - 3,089
  - 2,198
    8,133
  _______
```

578.
```
    8,054
  - 2,550
    7,601
  - 1,530
  _______
```

579.
```
    6,265
    4,569
  - 3,706
  - 3,010
  _______
```

580.
```
    7,751
  - 4,387
    6,298
  - 2,459
  _______
```

581.
```
    8,873
    2,665
  - 3,669
  - 3,134
  _______
```

582.
```
    8,360
  - 3,048
    8,550
  - 3,883
  _______
```

583.
```
    6,976
  - 2,452
    1,924
  - 2,839
  _______
```

584.
```
    6,241
  - 1,024
    2,206
  - 3,139
  _______
```

585.
```
    6,829
  - 3,109
    8,937
  - 3,223
  _______
```

586.
```
    5,786
  - 1,607
    7,282
  - 3,202
  _______
```

587.
```
    6,890
  - 2,042
  - 2,011
    5,012
  _______
```

588.
```
    5,993
  - 2,676
  - 2,267
    3,152
  _______
```

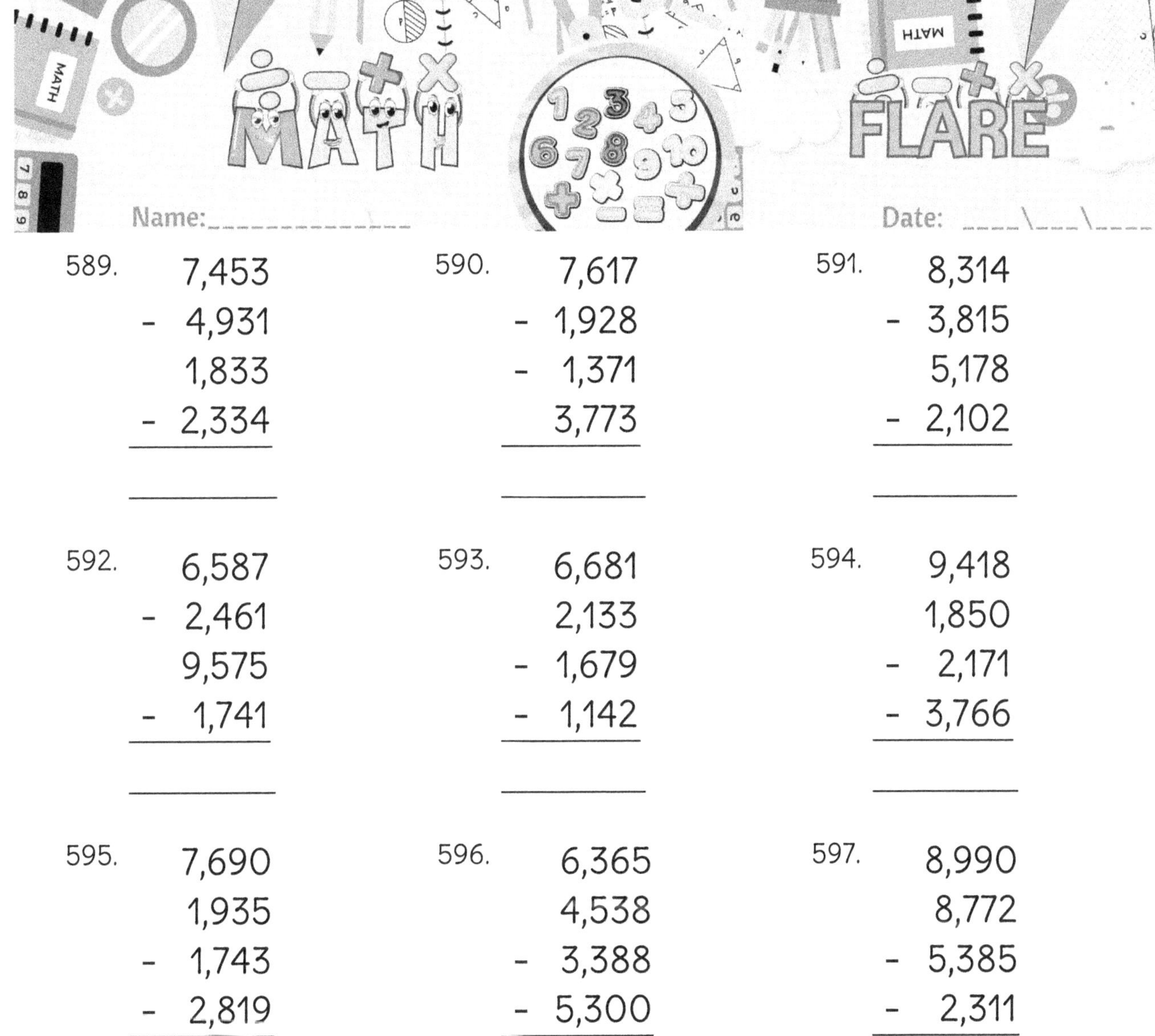

| 589. | 590. | 591. |
|---|---|---|
| 7,453<br>- 4,931<br>1,833<br>- 2,334 | 7,617<br>- 1,928<br>- 1,371<br>3,773 | 8,314<br>- 3,815<br>5,178<br>- 2,102 |
| 592. | 593. | 594. |
| 6,587<br>- 2,461<br>9,575<br>- 1,741 | 6,681<br>2,133<br>- 1,679<br>- 1,142 | 9,418<br>1,850<br>- 2,171<br>- 3,766 |
| 595. | 596. | 597. |
| 7,690<br>1,935<br>- 1,743<br>- 2,819 | 6,365<br>4,538<br>- 3,388<br>- 5,300 | 8,990<br>8,772<br>- 5,385<br>- 2,311 |
| 598. | 599. | 600. |
| 9,607<br>- 4,313<br>1,044<br>- 1,401 | 7,237<br>- 3,582<br>- 3,307<br>4,945 | 8,518<br>5,078<br>- 2,114<br>- 5,429 |

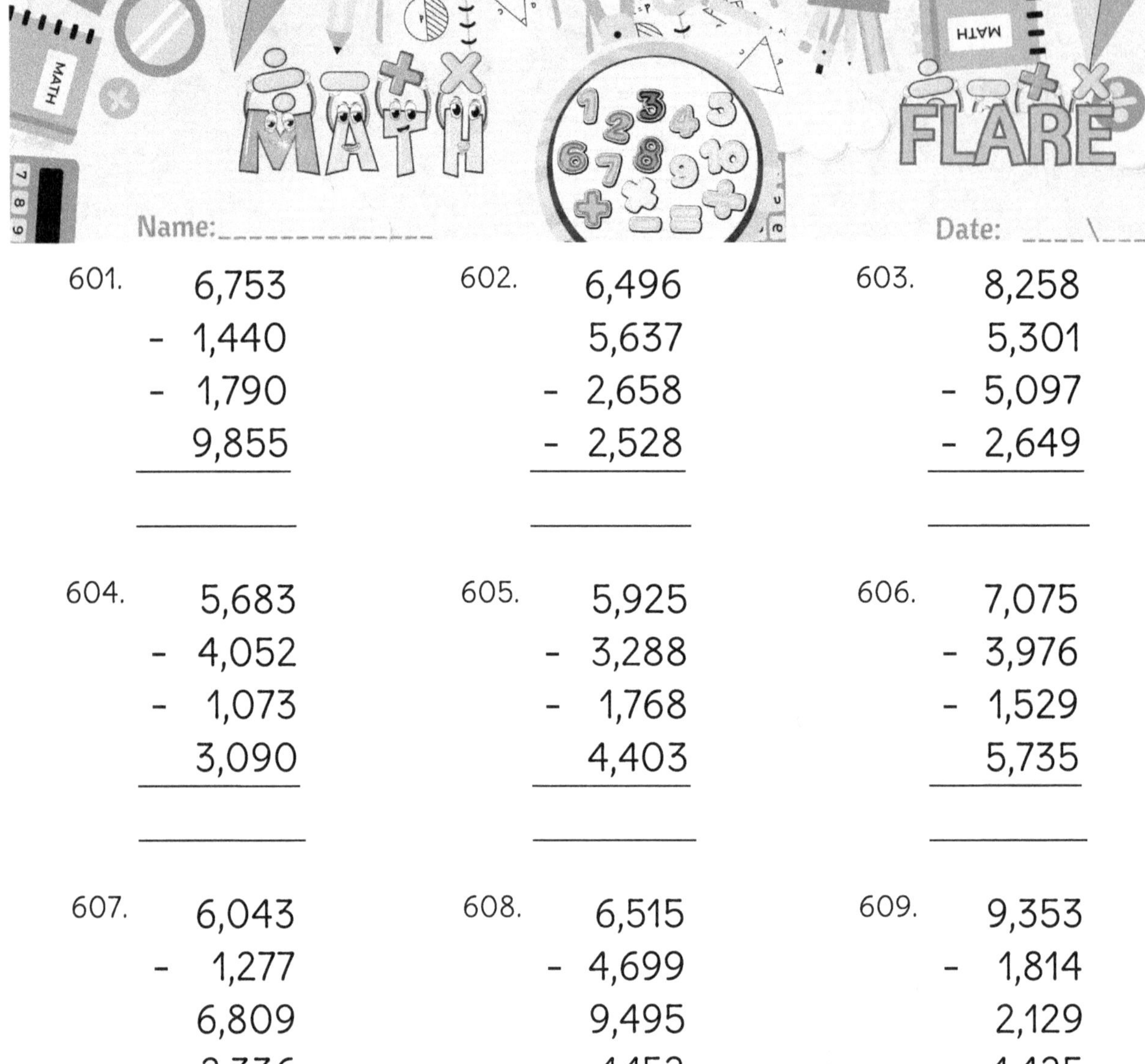

| | | |
|---|---|---|
| 601.  6,753<br>− 1,440<br>− 1,790<br>  9,855 | 602.  6,496<br>  5,637<br>− 2,658<br>− 2,528 | 603.  8,258<br>  5,301<br>− 5,097<br>− 2,649 |
| 604.  5,683<br>− 4,052<br>− 1,073<br>  3,090 | 605.  5,925<br>− 3,288<br>− 1,768<br>  4,403 | 606.  7,075<br>− 3,976<br>− 1,529<br>  5,735 |
| 607.  6,043<br>− 1,277<br>  6,809<br>− 2,336 | 608.  6,515<br>− 4,699<br>  9,495<br>− 1,152 | 609.  9,353<br>− 1,814<br>  2,129<br>− 1,425 |
| 610.  6,443<br>  5,922<br>− 4,303<br>− 2,172 | 611.  7,727<br>− 3,856<br>  7,104<br>− 2,956 | 612.  9,215<br>− 3,872<br>  1,434<br>− 4,185 |

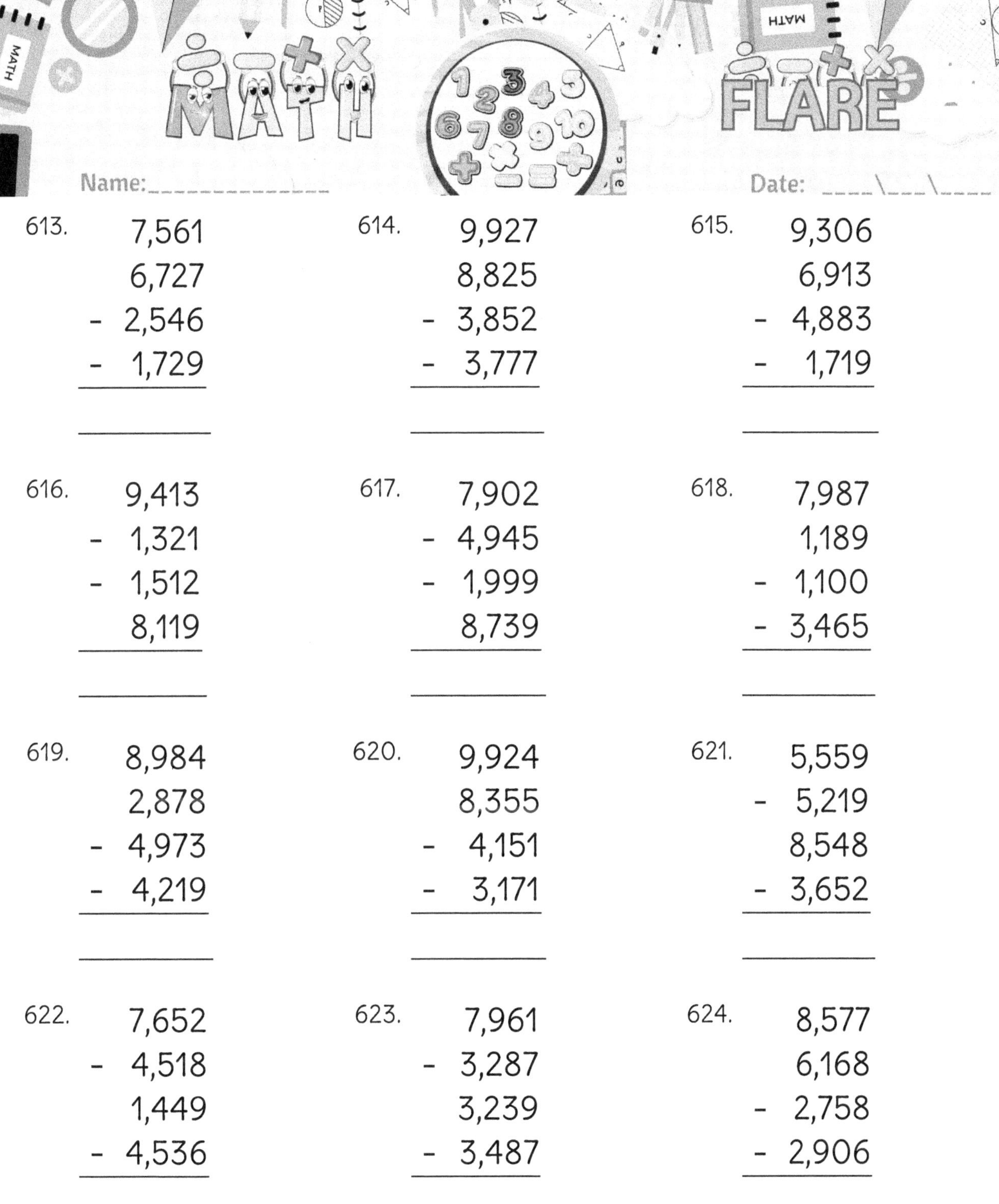



| | | |
|---|---|---|
| 613.  7,561<br>6,727<br>−  2,546<br>−  1,729 | 614.  9,927<br>8,825<br>−  3,852<br>−  3,777 | 615.  9,306<br>6,913<br>−  4,883<br>−  1,719 |
| 616.  9,413<br>−  1,321<br>−  1,512<br>8,119 | 617.  7,902<br>−  4,945<br>−  1,999<br>8,739 | 618.  7,987<br>1,189<br>−  1,100<br>−  3,465 |
| 619.  8,984<br>2,878<br>−  4,973<br>−  4,219 | 620.  9,924<br>8,355<br>−  4,151<br>−  3,171 | 621.  5,559<br>−  5,219<br>8,548<br>−  3,652 |
| 622.  7,652<br>−  4,518<br>1,449<br>−  4,536 | 623.  7,961<br>−  3,287<br>3,239<br>−  3,487 | 624.  8,577<br>6,168<br>−  2,758<br>−  2,906 |

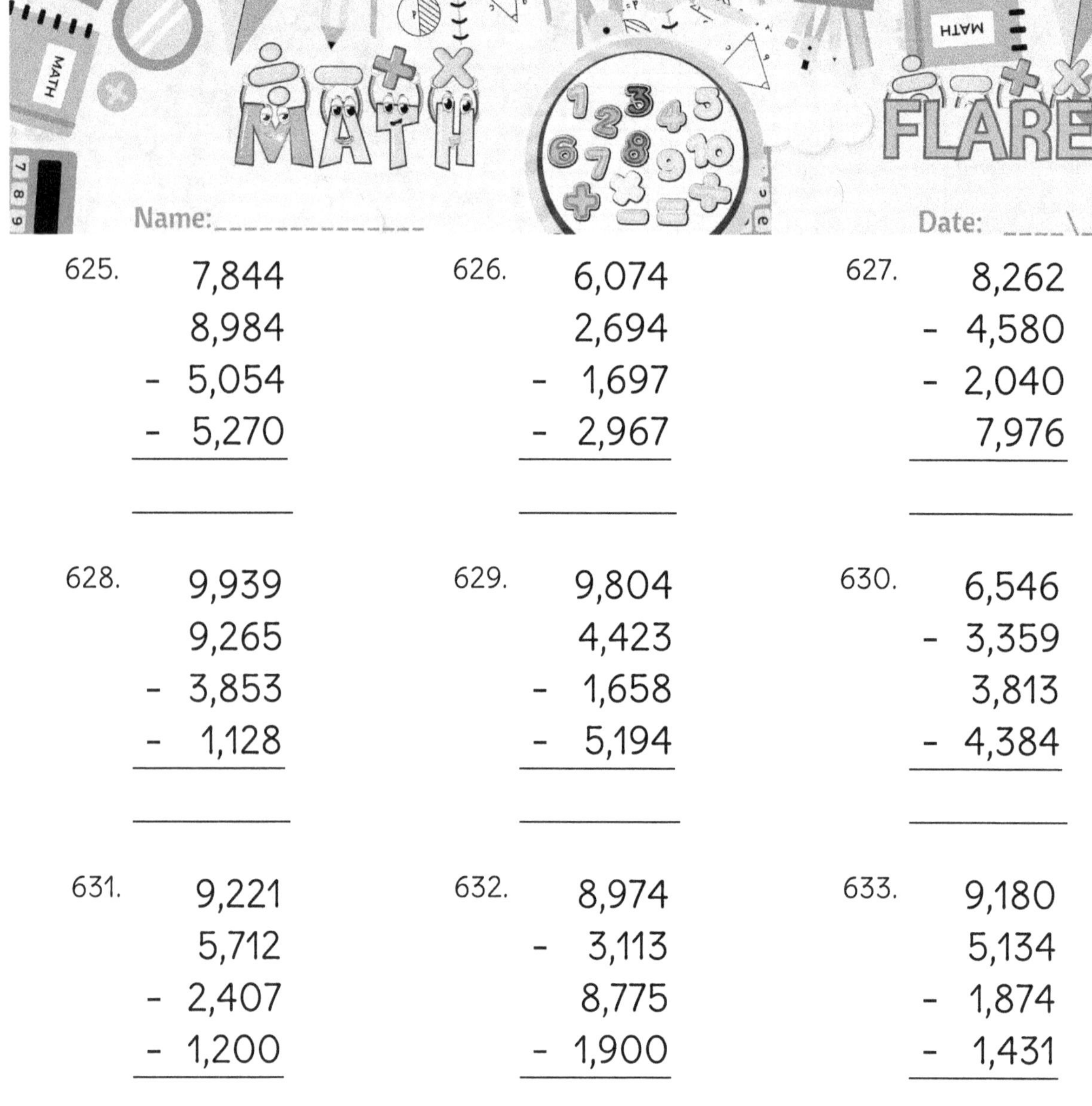

625.
7,844
8,984
- 5,054
- 5,270
_______

626.
6,074
2,694
- 1,697
- 2,967
_______

627.
8,262
- 4,580
- 2,040
7,976
_______

628.
9,939
9,265
- 3,853
- 1,128
_______

629.
9,804
4,423
- 1,658
- 5,194
_______

630.
6,546
- 3,359
3,813
- 4,384
_______

631.
9,221
5,712
- 2,407
- 1,200
_______

632.
8,974
- 3,113
8,775
- 1,900
_______

633.
9,180
5,134
- 1,874
- 1,431
_______

634.
9,623
- 4,381
4,192
- 4,713
_______

635.
9,021
4,614
- 5,389
- 4,072
_______

636.
7,272
3,472
- 1,001
- 3,829
_______

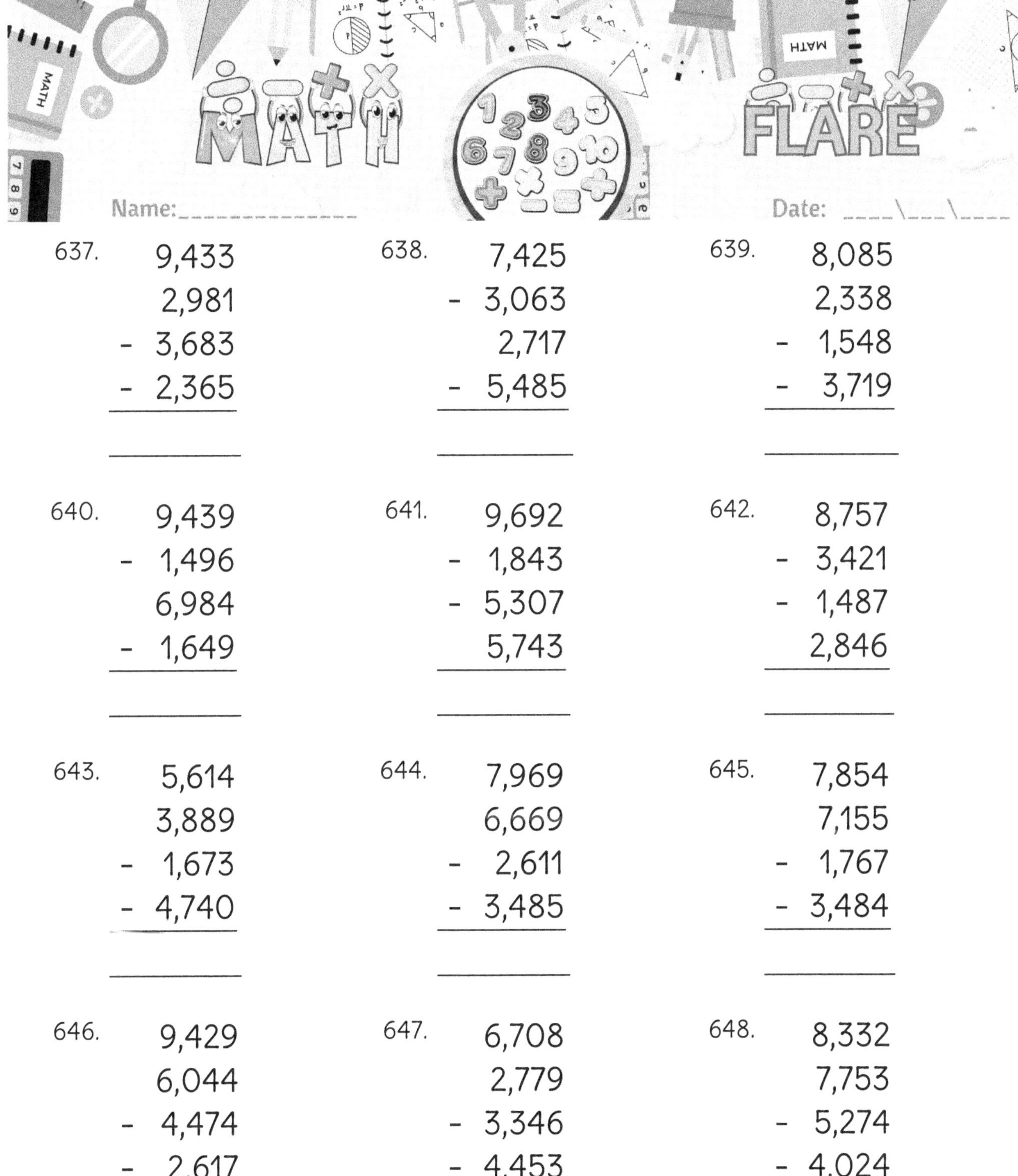



| | | |
|---|---|---|
| 637.    9,433<br>2,981<br>- 3,683<br>- 2,365 | 638.    7,425<br>- 3,063<br>2,717<br>- 5,485 | 639.    8,085<br>2,338<br>- 1,548<br>- 3,719 |
| 640.    9,439<br>- 1,496<br>6,984<br>- 1,649 | 641.    9,692<br>- 1,843<br>- 5,307<br>5,743 | 642.    8,757<br>- 3,421<br>- 1,487<br>2,846 |
| 643.    5,614<br>3,889<br>- 1,673<br>- 4,740 | 644.    7,969<br>6,669<br>- 2,611<br>- 3,485 | 645.    7,854<br>7,155<br>- 1,767<br>- 3,484 |
| 646.    9,429<br>6,044<br>- 4,474<br>- 2,617 | 647.    6,708<br>2,779<br>- 3,346<br>- 4,453 | 648.    8,332<br>7,753<br>- 5,274<br>- 4,024 |

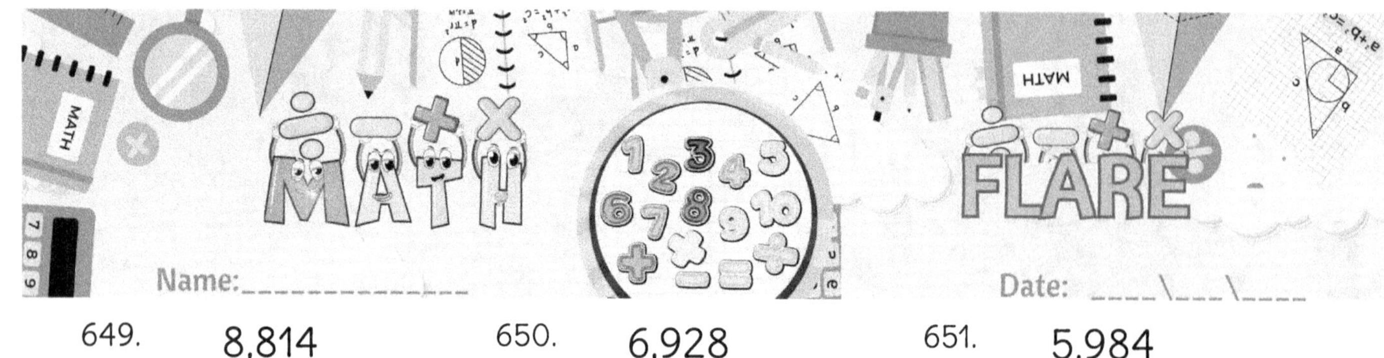


| 649. | 650. | 651. |
|---|---|---|
| 8,814<br>- 4,739<br>- 3,309<br>2,859 | 6,928<br>5,258<br>- 5,071<br>- 2,511 | 5,984<br>4,520<br>- 2,249<br>- 1,481 |
| 652. | 653. | 654. |
| 6,889<br>- 2,618<br>5,030<br>- 5,251 | 9,058<br>- 3,563<br>1,728<br>- 1,861 | 9,729<br>- 1,507<br>- 2,219<br>4,340 |
| 655. | 656. | 657. |
| 7,368<br>- 3,689<br>- 1,692<br>5,736 | 5,574<br>- 2,551<br>- 2,165<br>3,478 | 7,170<br>5,296<br>- 1,425<br>- 4,230 |
| 658. | 659. | 660. |
| 9,455<br>- 1,681<br>3,113<br>- 1,225 | 9,005<br>- 4,755<br>- 2,444<br>5,339 | 6,772<br>6,986<br>- 1,227<br>- 5,090 |

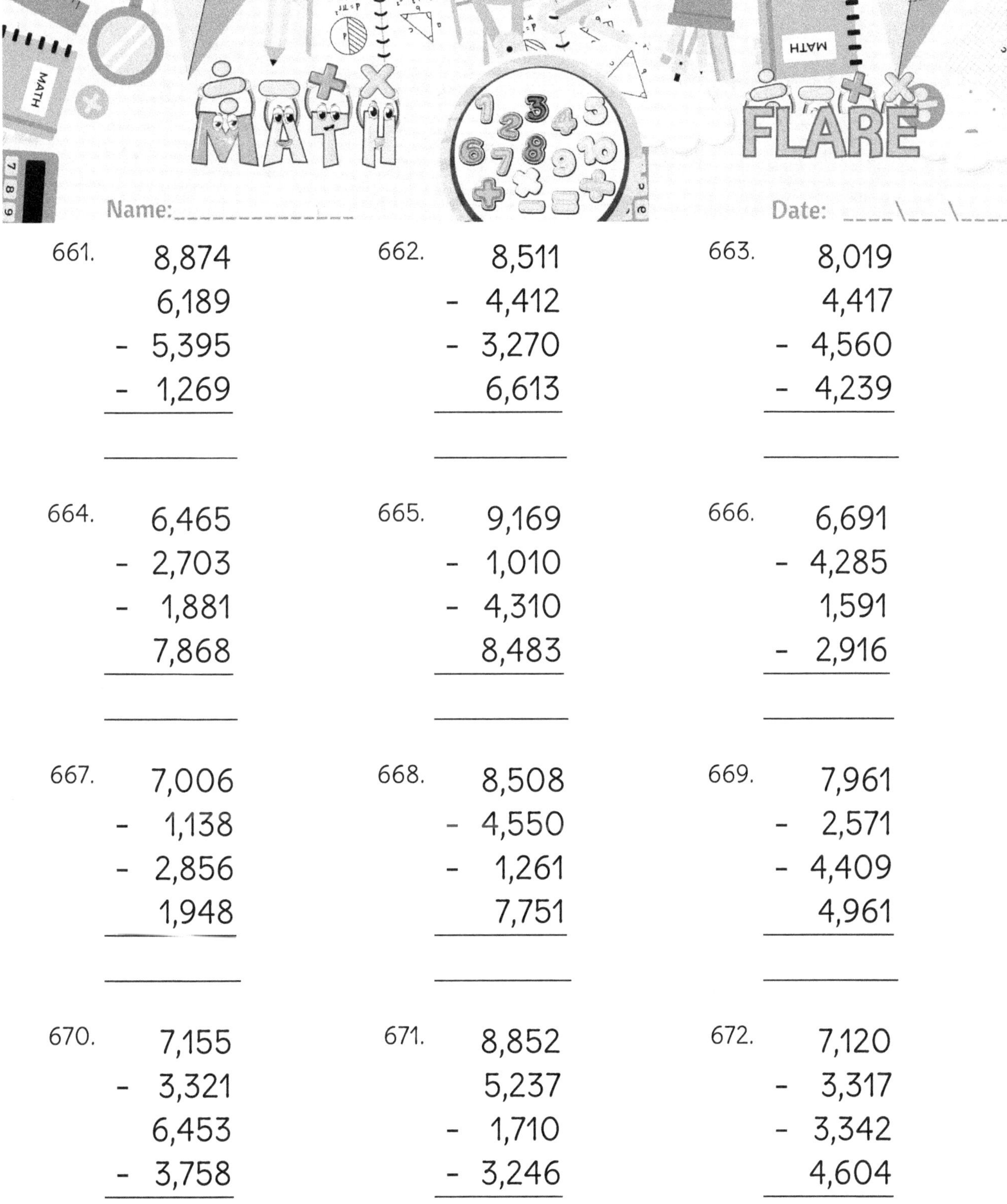

| | | |
|---|---|---|
| 661.    8,874<br>6,189<br>- 5,395<br>- 1,269 | 662.    8,511<br>- 4,412<br>- 3,270<br>6,613 | 663.    8,019<br>4,417<br>- 4,560<br>- 4,239 |
| 664.    6,465<br>- 2,703<br>- 1,881<br>7,868 | 665.    9,169<br>- 1,010<br>- 4,310<br>8,483 | 666.    6,691<br>- 4,285<br>1,591<br>- 2,916 |
| 667.    7,006<br>- 1,138<br>- 2,856<br>1,948 | 668.    8,508<br>- 4,550<br>- 1,261<br>7,751 | 669.    7,961<br>- 2,571<br>- 4,409<br>4,961 |
| 670.    7,155<br>- 3,321<br>6,453<br>- 3,758 | 671.    8,852<br>5,237<br>- 1,710<br>- 3,246 | 672.    7,120<br>- 3,317<br>- 3,342<br>4,604 |

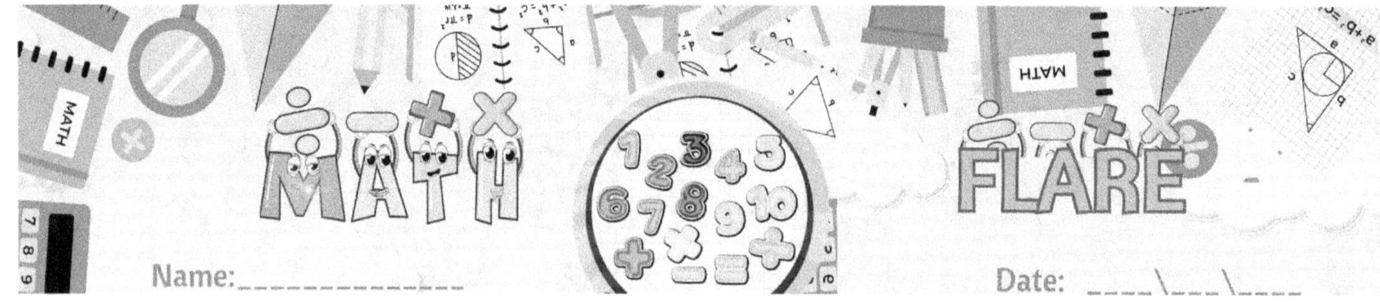

# Addition Word Problems

673. Zachary has 16 gloves. He receives 18 more gloves. How many gloves does he have now?

674. Mila has 4 headphones in a bag. If Mila adds 6 more headphones to the bag, how many headphones does Mila have in total?

675. The weight of an empty container is 3 pounds. If the container is filled with 14 pounds of calendars, what is the total weight of the container and its contents?

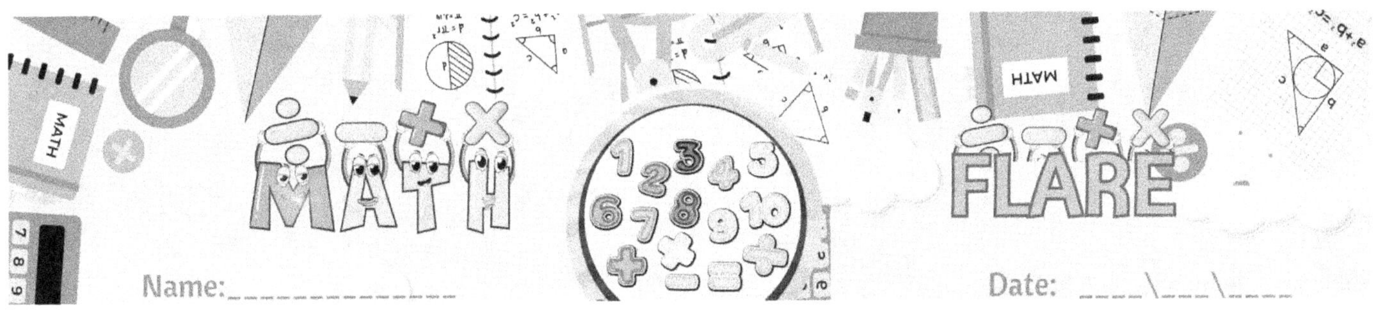


676. There are 12 parrots on a tree. 10 more parrots land on the tree. How many parrots are on the tree now?

677. There are 8 cats in the ground. 13 more cats come to play. How many cats are in the ground now?

678. Zoey has 1 cake. She gets 20 cakes from her friend. How many cakes does Zoey have now?

679. David bought a bag of flowers for 8 dollars. Later, David bought another bag of flowers for 5 dollars. How much money did David spend in total?

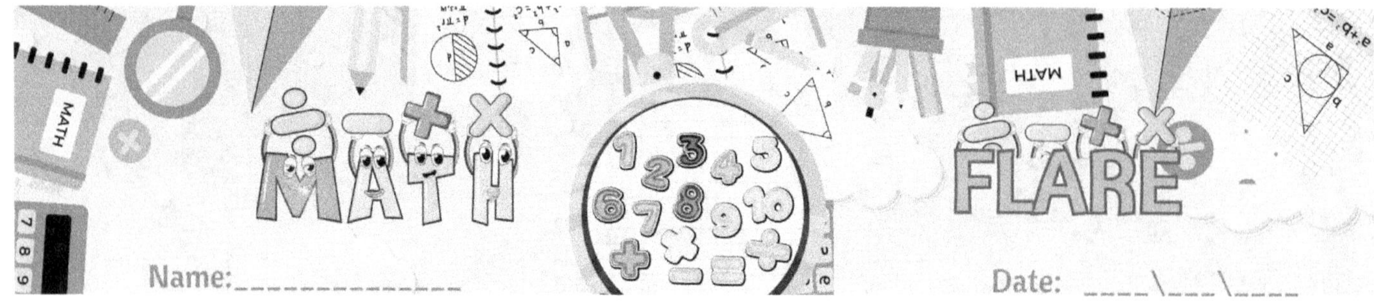



Name:_______________          Date: ____________

680. Logan has 6 flosses. He gets 14 more flosses. How many flosses does he have now?

681. Elizabeth has 13 liters of water in a container. She pours in 5 more liters of water. How much water is in the container now?

682. Madelyn planted 10 flowers in the morning and 20 flowers in the afternoon. How many flowers did Madelyn plant?

683. Dylan has 12 fish in an aquarium. If Dylan adds 15 more fish to the aquarium, how many fish will be in the aquarium in total?

**684.** Peyton baked 8 cakes yesterday and 8 cakes today. How many cakes did Peyton bake in total?

**685.** A basketball team scored 2 points in the first quarter and 11 points in the second quarter. What was the total score of the basketball team after the first half?

**686.** Colton spent 3 dollars on Monday and 1 dollars on Tuesday. How much money did Colton spend in total?

**687.** Elena walked 20 miles yesterday and 2 miles today. How many miles did Elena walk in total?

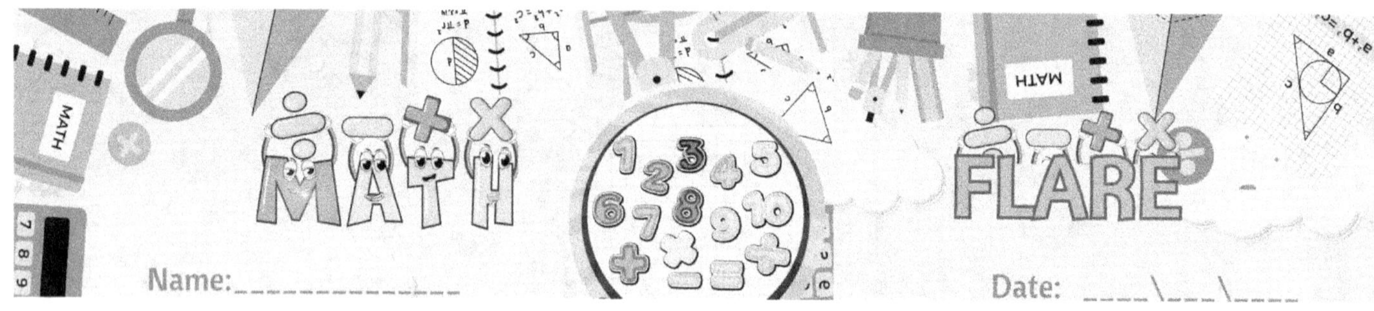



688. Kennedy wrote 6 pages of her book yesterday and 12 pages today. How many pages did she write in total?

689. There are 10 compasses in the room. 15 more compasses are brought in. How many compasses are in the room now?

690. Kai filled a tank with 17 gallons of gas and then added 8 more gallons. How many gallons of gas are in the tank now?

691. A soccer team scored 4 goals in the first half and 8 goals in the second half. What was the total score of the soccer team?

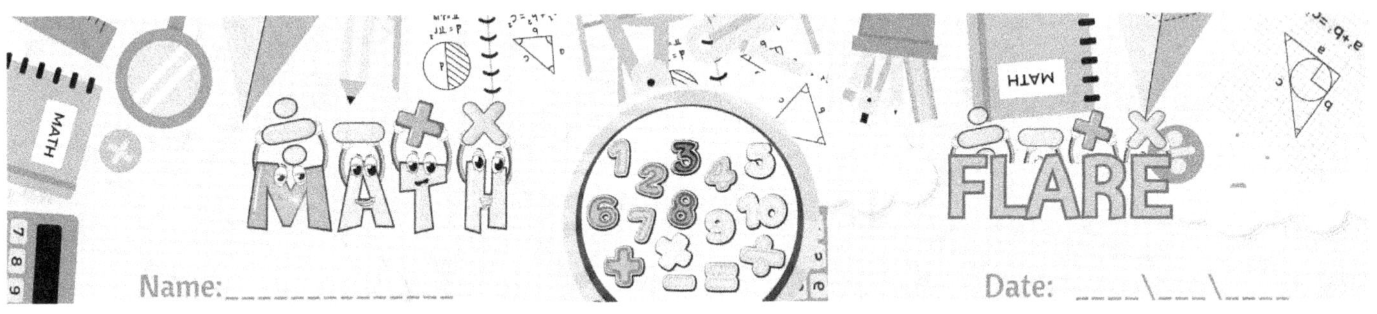


692. Skylar bought 13 scarves and later bought 7 scarves. How many scarves does Skylar have now?

693. Hazel bought pizzas with 17 slices. Later, Hazel bought some more pizzas with 12 slices. How many slices of pizzas does Hazel have in total?

694. Sebastian has 13 tissues and buys 16 more tissues. How many tissues does Sebastian have in total?

695. Arianna has 3 pianos. She gets 10 more pianos. How many pianos does Arianna have now?

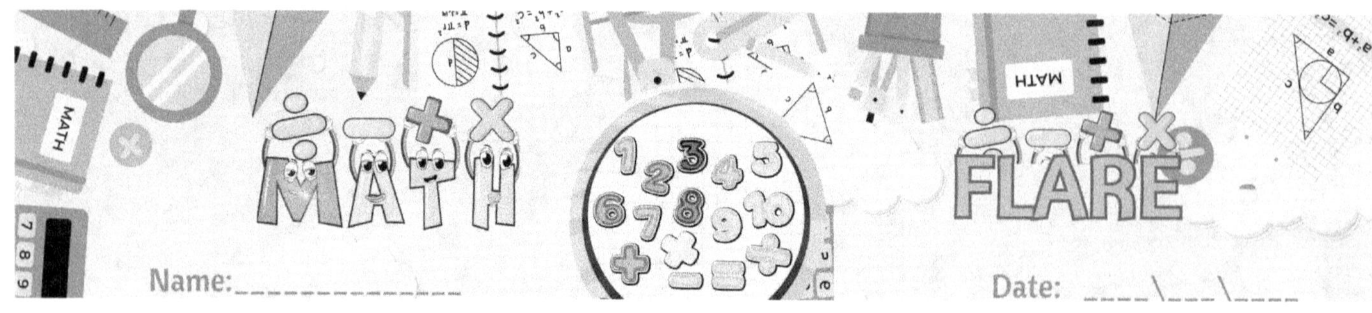


696. Roman had 19 dollars in the morning and earned 2 more dollars in the afternoon. How many dollars Roman have in total?

697. At the beginning of the week, there were 20 apples in the basket. By the end of the week, 14 more apples were added to the basket. How many apples are in the basket now?

698. A bakery sold 18 cupcakes in the morning and 8 cupcakes in the afternoon. How many cupcakes did the bakery sell in total?

699. Gemma has 18 lotions. She buys 6 more lotions at the store. How many lotions does Gemma have now?

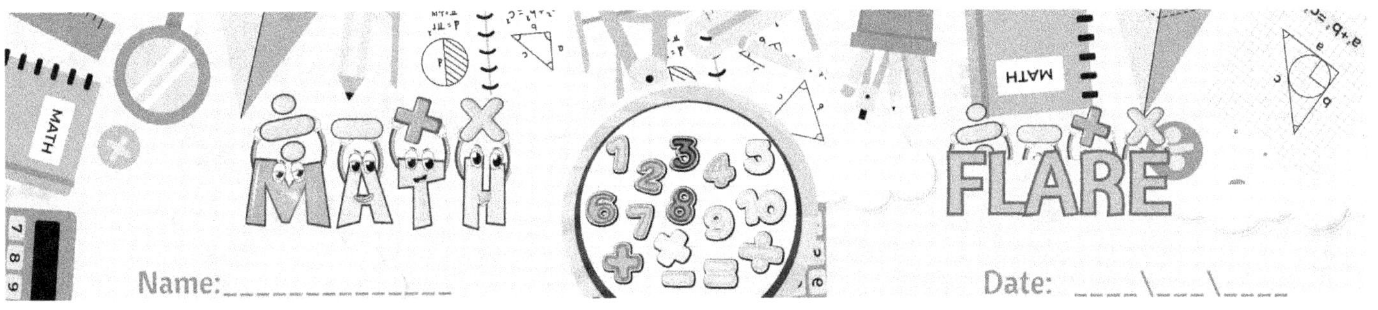


700. A machine has 11 parts. If 2 more parts are added, how many parts does the machine have now?

701. There are 11 crows on a tree. 16 more crows land on the tree. How many crows are on the tree now?

702. On Monday, Naomi solved 5 math problems, and on Tuesday, Naomi solved 13 problems. How many math problems did Naomi solve?

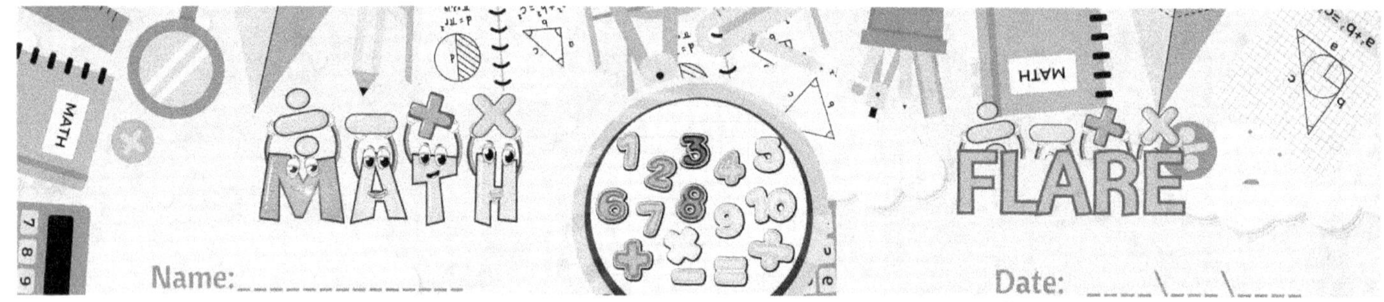


# Subtraction Word Problems

703. Zoey has 16 surgical masks in her collection. She gave 2 of them to her friend. How many surgical masks does Zoey have now?

704. There are 19 fish in a tank. If 1 leave, how many fish are left in the tank?

705. A box had 7 chocolates. Paisley ate 4 chocolates. How many chocolates are left in the box?

706. Bella bought syringes for 13 dollars. She received 13 dollars in change. How much did syringes cost?

707. A notebooks costs $14 and a pen costs $14. How much more expensive is the notebooks than the pen?

708. There are 15 turtles in a pond. If 10 leave, how many turtles are left in the pond?

709. There are 3 coins. 3 coins are blue and the rest are red. How many red coins are in the box?

Name:___________________   Date: _______________

710. Leo has 9 toothpastes in his collection. He sold 1 of them at a sale. How many toothpastes does he have left in his collection?

711. There are 11 fish in a pond. Genesis caught 6 fish. How many fish are left in the pond?

712. Sofia baked a 1 cookies. 1 of them were chocolate chip cookies and the rest were oatmeal raisin cookies. How many oatmeal raisin cookies did Sofia bake?

713. If breads costs 1 dollars and you have 1 dollars, how much more money do you need to buy it?

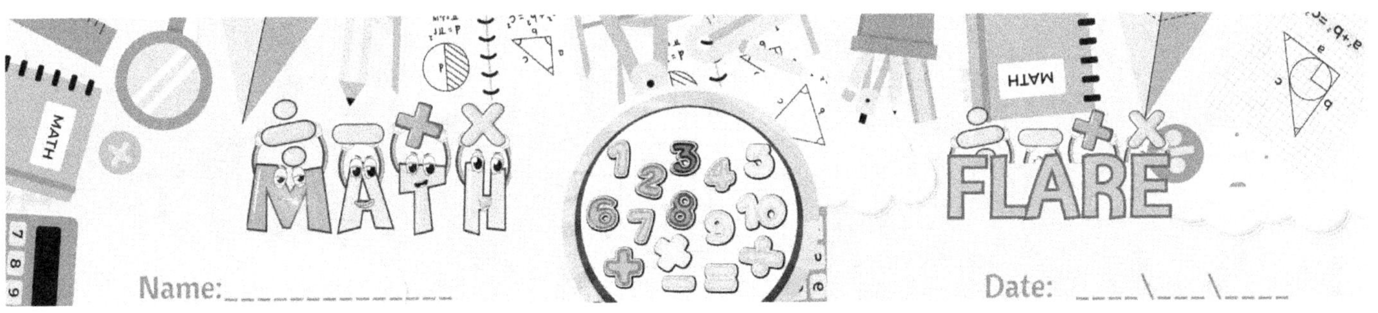


714. Cooper had 14 dollars. He spent 8 dollars on a books. How much money does Cooper have left?

715. Zara bought clocks for 5 dollars. She later returned some clocks and received a refund of 4 dollars. How much money did she end up spending on clocks?

716. A pack of gum had 10 pieces. Leah took 3 pieces of gum. How many pieces of gum are left in the pack?

717. Harper and Natalia went shopping for lotions. They had 19 dollars to spend but 8 dollars ended up being spent. How much money do they have left?

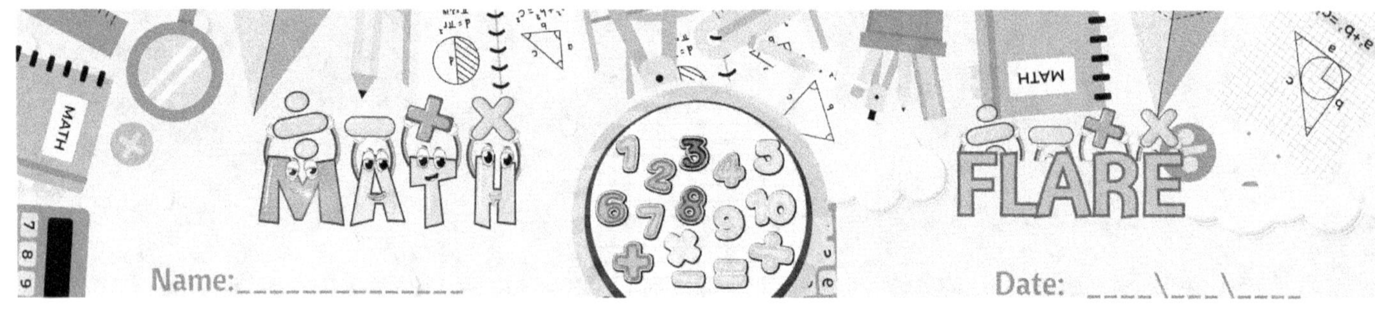


718. There are 3 dogs in a park. If 1 leave, how many dogs are left in the park?

719. Tissues originally cost 20 dollars, but it is now on sale for 8 dollars. How much money can you save by buying it on sale?

720. Lydia wants to buy chocolates, which costs 11 dollars. She has 9 dollars and plans to save the rest. How much more money does she need to save to buy chocolates?

721. Alexa has 13 thermometers. She lost 3 of them. How many thermometers does Alexa have left?

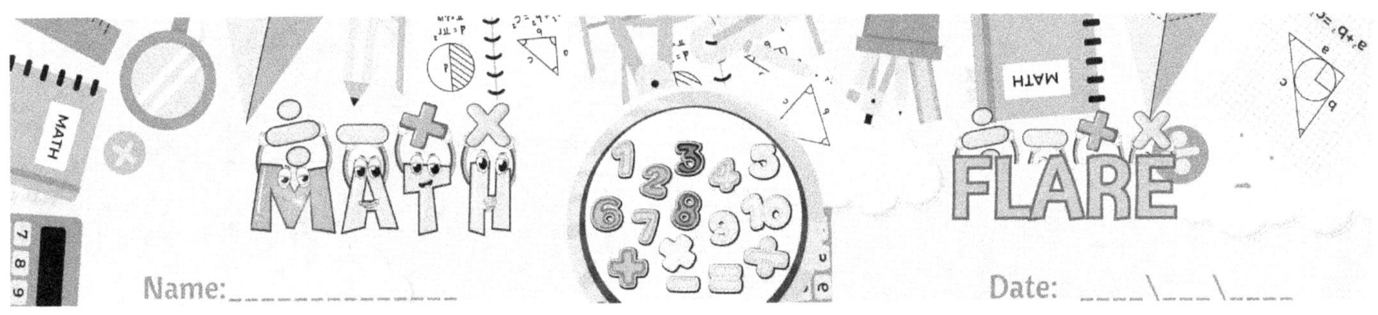


722. Ian is 1 years old and Ethan is 1 years old. What is the difference in their ages?

723. Isabella bought forks for 11 dollars but later found out it was on sale for 6 dollars less. How much did she overpay for forks?

724. Adam had 17 calculators. He gave 11 calculators to Genesis. How many calculators does Adam have left?

725. Nathan has 6 dollars. He needs to buy muffins that costs 8 dollars. How much money will he have left after buying the muffins?

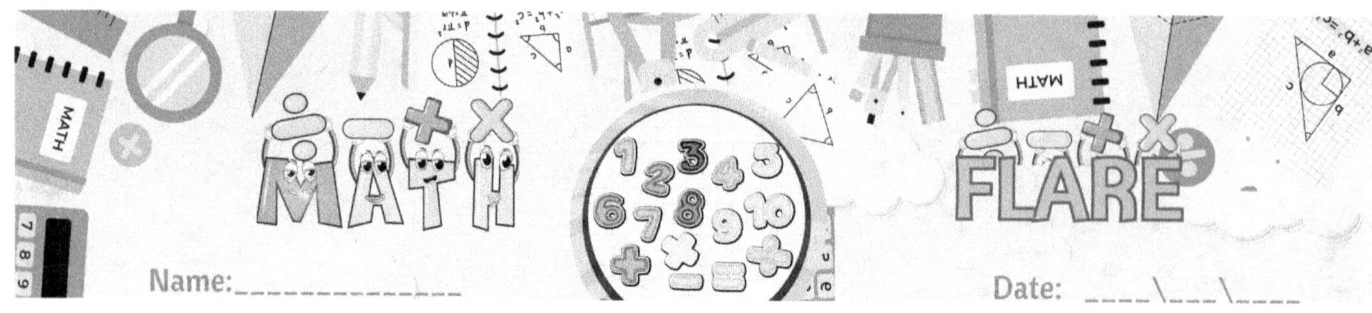


726. There were 10 students in a class. 7 of them were absent. How many students were present in the class?

727. Christian saved up 19 dollars to buy scalpels. He spent 18 dollars on it. How much money does he have left?

728. Luna has 13 gauzes. She gave 5 gauzes to Kennedy. How many gauzes does Luna have now?

729. A box of knives weighs 14 pounds. If you remove 4 pounds from it, how much does it weigh now?

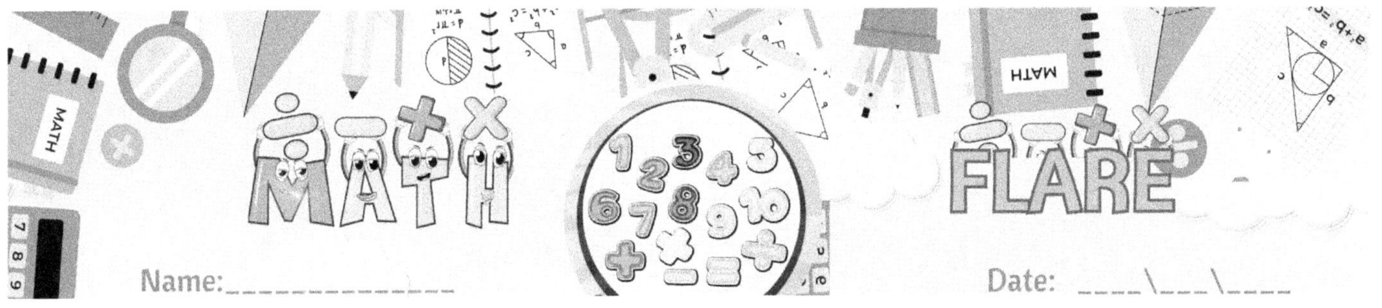


Name:_________________  Date: ____________

730. Julian has 3 cotton swabs. He traded 3 of them with his friend. How many cotton swabs does Julian have now?

731. If you have 6 rocks and you give away 6, how many rocks do you have left?

732. There are 17 rulers in a bag. Lila took 14 rulers out of the bag. How many rulers are still in the bag?

733. A pizza has 7 slices. Paisley ate 2 slices. How many slices of pizza are left?

# ANSWERS

## Page 1:  Addition with Regrouping

| | | | | |
|---|---|---|---|---|
| 1. 17,320 | 2. 12,120 | 3. 12,437 | 4. 15,350 | 5. 12,661 |
| 6. 12,210 | 7. 11,115 | 8. 12,171 | 9. 12,151 | 10. 14,230 |
| 11. 11,111 | 12. 12,161 | 13. 17,760 | 14. 14,331 | 15. 15,211 |
| 16. 19,420 | 17. 11,182 | 18. 11,111 | 19. 13,916 | 20. 12,460 |
| 21. 14,130 | 22. 11,263 | 23. 13,111 | 24. 11,113 | 25. 13,141 |
| 26. 11,481 | 27. 12,222 | 28. 12,746 | 29. 13,210 | 30. 11,262 |
| 31. 11,210 | 32. 12,241 | 33. 13,372 | 34. 11,711 | 35. 15,244 |
| 36. 13,520 | 37. 17,130 | 38. 13,470 | 39. 11,410 | 40. 11,640 |
| 41. 13,210 | 42. 13,430 | 43. 17,137 | 44. 15,122 | 45. 13,125 |
| 46. 14,215 | 47. 11,320 | 48. 11,232 | 49. 12,110 | 50. 11,116 |
| 51. 11,193 | 52. 12,513 | 53. 16,220 | 54. 13,410 | 55. 11,661 |
| 56. 12,150 | 57. 11,121 | 58. 19,610 | 59. 11,123 | 60. 13,211 |
| 61. 15,118 | 62. 11,130 | 63. 14,530 | 64. 11,315 | 65. 14,913 |
| 66. 15,141 | 67. 15,230 | 68. 13,322 | 69. 12,430 | 70. 11,350 |
| 71. 13,110 | 72. 14,111 | 73. 13,121 | 74. 12,250 | 75. 11,612 |
| 76. 11,311 | 77. 11,214 | 78. 12,254 | 79. 11,210 | 80. 15,152 |
| 81. 14,710 | 82. 11,530 | 83. 12,115 | 84. 14,412 | 85. 12,434 |
| 86. 15,150 | 87. 12,121 | 88. 11,720 | 89. 19,423 | 90. 12,111 |

91. 14,625    92. 11,210    93. 14,210    94. 12,240    95. 12,670

96. 11,150    97. 11,241    98. 11,161    99. 13,343    100. 11,327

## Page 6:  Subtraction with Regrouping

101. 759    102. 783    103. 2,889    104. 5,589    105. 1,665

106. 1,826    107. 739    108. 6,213    109. 1,689    110. 865

111. 4,356    112. 2,865    113. 879    114. 119    115. 266

116. 4,134    117. 3,868    118. 5,476    119. 1,329    120. 2,589

121. 2,779    122. 3,376    123. 1,679    124. 573    125. 2,827

126. 288    127. 1,874    128. 853    129. 4,569    130. 2,809

131. 389    132. 785    133. 6,869    134. 879    135. 1,884

136. 4,889    137. 889    138. 867    139. 2,886    140. 3,477

141. 2,389    142. 835    143. 888    144. 6,475    145. 477

146. 2,886    147. 826    148. 788    149. 1,588    150. 856

151. 1,887    152. 3,689    153. 5,877    154. 4,436    155. 782

156. 4,668    157. 3,871    158. 465    159. 1,869    160. 2,869

161. 679    162. 4,679    163. 148    164. 1,488    165. 1,589

166. 885    167. 3,652    168. 879    169. 5,858    170. 679

171. 3,889    172. 768    173. 682    174. 1,489    175. 3,757

176. 686    177. 857    178. 2,676    179. 6,787    180. 839

181. 679    182. 2,567    183. 3,762    184. 1,569    185. 558

186. 4,788    187. 467    188. 868    189. 379    190. 868

191. 788        192. 384        193. 2,389        194. 2,876        195. 589

196. 773

## Page 11:  Addition Unknown Number

197. 938     198. 189     199. 1,431     200. 472     201. 315     202. 798

203. 845     204. 1,261     205. 1,411     206. 936     207. 694     208. 711

209. 556     210. 1,210     211. 1,320     212. 896     213. 425     214. 1,140

215. 974     216. 1,821     217. 549     218. 1,650     219. 599     220. 783

221. 997     222. 1,210     223. 995     224. 988     225. 999     226. 491

227. 1,217     228. 1,150     229. 358     230. 1,311     231. 795     232. 343

233. 1,544     234. 446     235. 849     236. 1,140     237. 989     238. 998

239. 159     240. 979     241. 789     242. 1,221     243. 838     244. 1,230

245. 1,112     246. 633     247. 234     248. 987     249. 321     250. 985

251. 676     252. 559     253. 1,110     254. 313     255. 1,110     256. 776

257. 1,122     258. 1,181     259. 547     260. 1,312     261. 896     262. 951

263. 1,163     264. 998     265. 1,110     266. 291     267. 399     268. 681

269. 864     270. 811     271. 482     272. 1,282     273. 1,622     274. 535

275. 311     276. 285     277. 677     278. 1,132     279. 885     280. 996

281. 1,290     282. 1,428     283. 1,281     284. 999     285. 988     286. 686

287. 1,224     288. 1,215     289. 267     290. 131     291. 142     292. 1,314

293. 114     294. 827     295. 133     296. 229     297. 646     298. 1,123

Page 17:  Subtraction: Unknown Number

| | | | | | |
|---|---|---|---|---|---|
| 299. 241 | 300. 375 | 301. 493 | 302. 805 | 303. 222 | 304. 402 |
| 305. 654 | 306. 604 | 307. 96 | 308. 294 | 309. 582 | 310. 335 |
| 311. 98 | 312. 917 | 313. 693 | 314. 41 | 315. 397 | 316. 214 |
| 317. 170 | 318. 596 | 319. 199 | 320. 145 | 321. 294 | 322. 240 |
| 323. 125 | 324. 552 | 325. 665 | 326. 169 | 327. 471 | 328. 927 |
| 329. 289 | 330. 449 | 331. 200 | 332. 3 | 333. 572 | 334. 282 |
| 335. 9 | 336. 74 | 337. 517 | 338. 287 | 339. 575 | 340. 706 |
| 341. 94 | 342. 313 | 343. 110 | 344. 290 | 345. 190 | 346. 892 |
| 347. 107 | 348. 647 | 349. 276 | 350. 255 | 351. 839 | 352. 73 |
| 353. 365 | 354. 260 | 355. 381 | 356. 11 | 357. 489 | 358. 891 |
| 359. 728 | 360. 655 | 361. 605 | 362. 683 | 363. 33 | 364. 176 |
| 365. 522 | 366. 458 | 367. 120 | 368. 848 | 369. 908 | 370. 281 |
| 371. 368 | 372. 127 | 373. 300 | 374. 146 | 375. 226 | 376. 185 |
| 377. 189 | 378. 936 | 379. 360 | 380. 481 | 381. 390 | 382. 283 |
| 383. 929 | 384. 726 | 385. 975 | 386. 911 | 387. 909 | 388. 600 |
| 389. 325 | 390. 527 | 391. 552 | 392. 71 | 393. 109 | 394. 741 |
| 395. 539 | 396. 679 | 397. 749 | 398. 268 | 399. 391 | 400. 872 |
| 401. 962 | 402. 671 | 403. 127 | 404. 844 | | |

Page 23:  Addition (3 Addends)

405. 15,396    406. 16,523    407. 21,826    408. 20,266    409. 18,144

410. 7,509       411. 17,200      412. 13,122      413. 11,938      414. 24,793

415. 15,377      416. 18,599      417. 12,617      418. 16,098      419. 14,911

420. 25,017      421. 23,171      422. 19,116      423. 18,268      424. 25,862

425. 18,708      426. 17,308      427. 17,405      428. 20,830      429. 21,672

430. 18,379      431. 18,244      432. 23,390      433. 13,245      434. 15,516

435. 13,843      436. 21,425      437. 17,329      438. 23,296      439. 21,375

440. 13,812      441. 16,288      442. 11,872      443. 12,805      444. 19,866

445. 21,341      446. 20,012      447. 21,894      448. 15,179      449. 5,142

450. 9,270       451. 27,030      452. 18,462      453. 15,236      454. 12,806

455. 14,859      456. 18,044      457. 12,135      458. 13,067      459. 16,510

460. 15,455      461. 5,359       462. 17,129      463. 21,811      464. 10,771

465. 14,003      466. 13,640      467. 19,064      468. 12,582      469. 24,926

470. 13,619      471. 22,600      472. 14,462      473. 20,765      474. 9,910

475. 24,063      476. 20,335      477. 17,570      478. 16,253      479. 22,677

480. 13,652      481. 18,112      482. 16,538      483. 12,774      484. 16,535

485. 10,957      486. 14,918      487. 16,063      488. 9,686       489. 18,329

490. 14,607      491. 19,688      492. 19,753      493. 19,141      494. 21,589

495. 20,186      496. 19,197      497. 22,764      498. 13,624      499. 20,972

500. 22,849      501. 13,605      502. 7,968       503. 18,059      504. 14,825

505. 12,577      506. 18,372      507. 10,083      508. 10,154      509. 13,411

510. 11,915      511. 14,895      512. 16,373      513. 21,767      514. 18,233

515. 8,876    516. 17,267    517. 11,582    518. 20,126    519. 19,765

520. 17,729   521. 6,235     522. 18,987    523. 19,672    524. 17,632

525. 11,826   526. 16,960    527. 11,043    528. 27,408

## Page 31:   Multiple Operations: Addition Subtraction

529. 7,429    530. 3,679     531. 8,315     532. 9,277     533. 9,507

534. 9,114    535. 1,016     536. 7,072     537. 4,592     538. 1,819

539. 8,747    540. 14,642    541. 4,798     542. 7,487     543. 4,578

544. 1,471    545. 5,041     546. 10,369    547. 6,635     548. 4,885

549. 5,338    550. 14,834    551. 5,896     552. 7,924     553. 8,578

554. 8,978    555. 5,641     556. 4,072     557. 3,356     558. 9,999

559. 3,201    560. 3,363     561. 11,161    562. 4,040     563. 10,093

564. 14,452   565. 5,681     566. 8,339     567. 6,710     568. 8,629

569. 5,322    570. 8,028     571. 8,054     572. 6,416     573. 9,257

574. 12,252   575. 6,852     576. 1,401     577. 11,781    578. 11,575

579. 4,118    580. 7,203     581. 4,735     582. 9,979     583. 3,609

584. 4,284    585. 9,434     586. 8,259     587. 7,849     588. 4,202

589. 2,021    590. 8,091     591. 7,575     592. 11,960    593. 5,993

594. 5,331    595. 5,063     596. 2,215     597. 10,066    598. 4,937

599. 5,293    600. 6,053     601. 13,378    602. 6,947     603. 5,813

604. 3,648    605. 5,272     606. 7,305     607. 9,239     608. 10,159

609. 8,243    610. 5,890     611. 8,019     612. 2,592     613. 10,013

614. 11,123     615. 9,617     616. 14,699     617. 9,697     618. 4,611

619. 2,670     620. 10,957     621. 5,236     622. 47     623. 4,426

624. 9,081     625. 6,504     626. 4,104     627. 9,618     628. 14,223

629. 7,375     630. 2,616     631. 11,326     632. 12,736     633. 11,009

634. 4,721     635. 4,174     636. 5,914     637. 6,366     638. 1,594

639. 5,156     640. 13,278     641. 8,285     642. 6,695     643. 3,090

644. 8,542     645. 9,758     646. 8,382     647. 1,688     648. 6,787

649. 3,625     650. 4,604     651. 6,774     652. 4,050     653. 5,362

654. 10,343     655. 7,723     656. 4,336     657. 6,811     658. 9,662

659. 7,145     660. 7,441     661. 8,399     662. 7,442     663. 3,637

664. 9,749     665. 12,332     666. 1,081     667. 4,960     668. 10,448

669. 5,942     670. 6,529     671. 9,133     672. 5,065

## Page 43:  Addition Word Problems

673. 34     674. 10     675. 17     676. 22     677. 21     678. 21     679. 13

680. 20     681. 18     682. 30     683. 27     684. 16     685. 13     686. 4

687. 22     688. 18     689. 25     690. 25     691. 12     692. 20     693. 29

694. 29     695. 13     696. 21     697. 34     698. 26     699. 24     700. 13

701. 27     702. 18

## Page 51:  Subtraction Word Problems

703. 14     704. 18     705. 3     706. 0     707. 0     708. 5     709. 0     710. 8

711. 5     712. 0     713. 0     714. 6     715. 1     716. 7     717. 11     718. 2

719. 12     720. 2     721. 10     722. 0     723. 5     724. 6     725. 2     726. 3

727. 1     728. 8     729. 10     730. 0     731. 0     732. 3     733. 5